Parchment Craft

Carla Larter

The Art of Crafts

First published in 1999 by
The Crowood Press Ltd
Ramsbury, Marlborough
Wiltshire SN8 2HR

British Library Cataloguing in Publication Data

A catalogue record for this book is available from the British Library.

ISBN 1 86126 214 0

Typeset by D & N Publishing
Membury Business Park, Lambourn Woodlands
Hungerford, Berkshire.

Printed and bound by Leo Paper Products, China.

Contents

Introduction

When I was asked to write a book on the basics of parchment craft, my first thoughts were that I was greatly honoured, but could I pull it off?

The most daunting challenge was to write an introduction. How can I describe this beautiful craft? Let me begin by telling you that it is not as daunting as it may seem. It offers anyone with just a hint of an artistic nature the chance to become, or to behave like, a real artist. With some basic knowledge, this craft can give much pleasure to creative people.

Parchment craft is an ancient craft that uses a wide variety of techniques to create beautiful, personal items, which are always individual to the maker. In the old days, parchment work, like leather work, was kept rather plain and simple, enhanced with natural inks, gold leaf, perforating and embossing. The craft is thought to have originated in Spain, in the days before Christopher Columbus sailed for the New World. It was taken to the Americas by the Church of Spain, in the wake of Columbus, and it is still taught in convent schools in Latin America to this day.

The craft is practised today in much the same way as it was in ancient times. Although various changes and new tools have been introduced, and the craft is now a culmination of techniques learnt throughout the centuries, with every culture adding something of its own character, it is fundamentally the same craft.

Originally, parchment craft was primarily used for embellishing religious works; today it is mainly used for making greetings cards, bookmarks, little gift cards, boxes, and so on.

The techniques of parchment craft are intriguing. They can be kept simple, but still produce impressive results. When the simpler techniques have been mastered, the student will soon be able to adopt more intricate methods. The lace work, for which this craft is best known, is particularly enchanting.

At demonstrations, or at our craft shop, I am often asked if parchment craft is an expensive hobby to begin. In fact, it is relatively inexpensive. The beginner will need parchment paper, a handful of tools, an embossing pad, inks for tracing, and, most importantly, his or her own inspired application.

When people say that this craft looks too difficult for them, I tell them that this is exactly what I said when I began a few years ago. Since then, I have developed my own style, and I am confident that, by learning a few tricks of the trade, you will be able to enjoy yourself as much as I do. I hope to give you here an insight into the right kind of working environment, the tools, and the various ways the techniques can be executed, using photographs, illustrations and step-by-step instructions. The illustrations, which show how to use the shading techniques, will also help you with the embossing, and will give you some ideas on how to paint on parchment paper, using felt-tip pens and ink.

One of my main aims is to inspire you; I wish you success in this craft, and as much pleasure as I have enjoyed.

1 Workspace & Equipment

YOUR WORKING SET-UP

As the work involved in parchment craft is of a very fine nature, it is imperative that you have a good supply of light. You should also make sure that the chair you are sitting on is at the right height compared with the height of your table. The table top should be at elbow level. Your chair should be comfortable and, if possible, adjustable. It is important to sit in an upright position – this is not only better for your back, but it also gives you more control over your hand.

To ensure that your working space is stable, do not have a cloth on the table. Use a large piece of board to protect the table top against damage, not only from spilt ink, but also during perforating, when there is a risk of the needle penetrating deeper than the thickness of the perforating pad. I use a sloping drawing board for this purpose, as this helps to keep my back straight and thus prevents

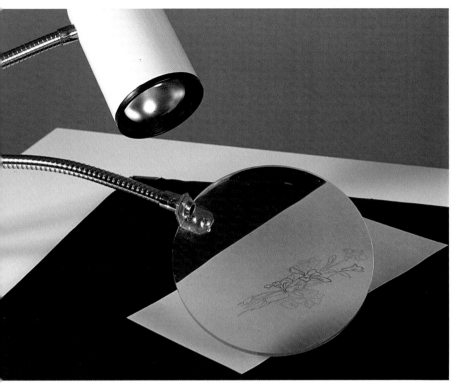

PAPYRUS TO PARCHMENT PAPER

The origins of parchment craft lie way back, before the birth of Christ. It is, in fact, known that parchment was used as long ago as 1500 BC.

The word 'parchment' is derived from the name of the ancient city of Pergamum. During the Attalid Dynasty, the Greek rulers of Pergamum, in north-west Asia, dedicated themselves to making their city a successor to Athens in its arts and culture. Pergamum became famous for its architecture, its parchment books and its vast library. The ruins of the acropolis of the ancient city, the site of which is close to the modern-day Turkish town of Bergama, may still be visited.

Before parchment, early books were made by using various materials, including leaves, bark, linen, silk, clay, leather and papyrus. Papyrus was a type of paper made by the ancient Egyptians, by gluing together about twenty sheets of the pith of a paper-reed plant. Parchments of kidskin, calfskin or lambskin, known as vellum, were used from the beginning of the fourth century, often rolled into scrolls. The five books of Moses were always written in Hebrew on vellum. (In modern times, the term 'vellum' describes a thick, specially treated, high-quality paper that resembles the fine parchment.)

The paper used today for parchment craft has been treated with special oily compounds, to give it the suppleness that is needed whilst embossing. Because of this treatment, it will not absorb inks or paints in the way that other papers do. One side of the paper is slightly rougher than the other; the rough side is usually used for tracing and painting, and the smooth side is used for embossing.

With practice, you will be able to feel this difference between the rough and

neck strain. Alternatively, you can place a flat board on a small beanbag, or on a couple of empty filing folders.

For the finest work, such as perforating, you may wish to use a magnifier. The best way to do this is to have the area you are working on showing through the upper third of the magnifying glass.

As this craft is highly addictive and, therefore, rather time-consuming, I would advise you to take regular breaks. When I start to feel the strain, I usually make myself a drink and walk round the house, contemplating my next step. I also like to wander round the garden – nature is a wonderful source of inspiration, and you may begin to look at it differently once you are involved in this craft. You will really appreciate the colours, and the shapes of petals and leaves, and will start to realize how important it is to show movement when painting. A good appreciation of nature will also be useful when you begin to learn the art of embossing.

the smooth sides, by holding a sheet of parchment paper with both hands, and gently running your fingertips over both sides. You should detect a slight variance in smoothness. If you cannot feel this, try placing the paper on the palms of your hands, and wiggling the paper with your fingers. The moisture of your hands will influence the fibres in the paper, and make the sheet curl.

The hollow side is the rough side of the paper, and this is the side you trace on.

The weight of most parchment paper is usually 150 gsm (grams per square metre). For boxes, lampshades, bookmarks or large cards, there is also a heavier paper available, at 200 gsm. This paper comes in a variety of colours, giving the so-called 'white work' a totally different aspect.

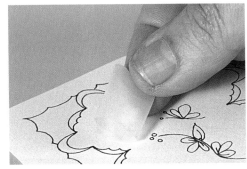

OTHER EQUIPMENT

Patterns

Ready-made patterns are available in packs and books, and are used to trace designs on to the parchment paper. (You do not have to be an artist to enjoy parchment craft, and this kind of 'cheating' is allowed!)

Sticky Tape/Magnetic Board

Low-tack sticky tape is used to adhere a sheet of parchment paper to the pattern. Take a couple of small pieces of tape, fold each piece in three with the sticky side out. Place these sticky rolls on to the pattern in strategic places, but not on the design itself.

This type of tape is easily removed without tearing either the parchment paper or the design, and it can be used again and again.

Alternatively, you may wish to use a magnetic board, which has two magnetic strips to hold your work in place.

Ink

Coloured liquids were used in ancient times for writing, drawing and printing. The traditional colour was blue; later, a permanent black was used, which was made from oxidized metals. Ink was originally produced from tannic acid, and gallic acid. The inks used today are based on synthetic dyes.

WHITE INK

A white ink with a chalky consistency is used to trace off the pattern. Give the bottle of ink a good shake before use, and use only a little ink at a time for tracing. Clean the nib of your mapping pen at regular intervals. First, wipe the nib on a piece of paper kitchen towel, then rinse in water, and shake off the excess, taking care not to splash any drops of water on to the parchment paper, as it will blister. Dry the nib before refilling it with ink.

Because this ink is relatively thick, you will need to trace as thinly as possible. The best results are achieved by holding the pen in a vertical position, and without applying any pressure. The nib is finely pointed, but rather flexible; holding the pen like this will keep the tips of the nib together, and should enable you to acquire a fine, thin line. If you hold the pen horizontally, the nib will splay, resulting in a much thicker

line, which will be hard to conceal whilst embossing.

Practise drawing some straight lines, curls, zigzags, and small and large circles on a spare piece of paper, trying to make them as thin as possible.

COLOURED INKS

These inks are used for tracing with a mapping pen, and also for painting with a brush. As these inks are thinner, take care not to press on the mapping pen whilst tracing; aim to 'float' the pen instead.

METALLIC INKS

These inks are used for tracing designs, for line work, and for highlights. I use the steel-nib pen for metallic inks, because the nib is larger, retaining more ink, and is slightly wider at the tip, which gives a broader outline. For highlights, use the smaller mapping pen; the intention is to refine the character of certain areas in the design, so the line should not be too prominent.

PEARLESCENT INKS

These contain acrylic, and can also be used for tracing with a mapping pen, or painting with a brush. They are water-based but need a good stir, before and during use.

Ink Pen

The earliest form of pen, a brush pen, was made by simply chewing the end of a reed, and was used by the Egyptians about 3000 BC. Some 200 years later, the Greeks replaced this with the reed pen, cutting a slit in the end of a reed at an angle, rather like a modern nib. This instrument was more suitable for writing the newly developed Greek alphabet. It was superseded by an implement made from the flight feathers of the goose or other large bird, cut nib-like; this proved better for its purpose, but it was awkward to use and needed frequent attention. It survived well into the eighteenth century, when the metal nib was invented.

A mapping pen is used to trace the design with ink on to the parchment paper. It need not be too expensive; I use a Conte No.1770, with a Conte nib for the normal ink, and an old-fashioned steel nib for the metallic inks.

New pens often have an oily surface, and this is often the reason why a new nib refuses to write. This can be remedied by washing the pen in hot soapy water.

After using the pen with ink, clean and dry the nib thoroughly. Do not store the nib inside the holder, otherwise you may have a problem with rust forming.

Embossing Tools

Parchment paper is a flexible material, made in sheets from vegetable fibres (such as wood pulp). In embossing, the paper is raised in relief by gently rubbing, with ball-pointed tools, over the paper, which is on a soft pad. This rubbing will stretch the fibres in the paper, and enlarge the area, having much the same effect as a rolling pin on pastry. Pressing too hard will crack the parchment paper, so you should take it easy, and aim gently to stretch it further. The colour of the paper will change with the rubbing from greyish to whitish and then, depending on the kind of result you want, to a brilliant, shiny white.

Some embossing work may be done with a single- or double-needle tool, or with specialized decorating tools.

Different-sized embossing tools produce different colour effects, as follows:

◆ fine stylus; stretches the fibres only a little, making the paper white;

◆ extra-small; stretches the fibres a little more, making the paper whitish;

◆ small ball; stretches a wider area in the fibres, making the paper greyish white;

◆ large ball; stretches a wide area in the fibres, making the paper light grey.

Using the wrong end of an embossing tool can give a soft effect to the work; it can also be used to pre-stretch a large area, prior to the embossing proper.

By practising with all the different tools on a spare piece of parchment paper, you will get the feel of them, and also see their different effects. Embossing repeatedly over the same area will make the colour of the paper increasingly white.

Embossing Pad

The effect of stretching the fibres in parchment paper, to raise the paper in relief after tracing, cannot be achieved on a hard, smooth surface. It needs to be done on a soft surface, such as an embossing pad. This usually consists of a piece of board with a plastic cover, and interlaced with a thin layer of foam rubber.

Perforating Mat

This mat is approximately 10mm thick, made of compressed fibres, such as felt

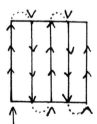
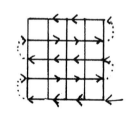

Directions of embossing

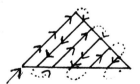
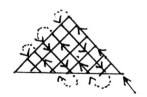
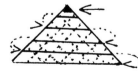

Finish with contour

or foam rubber. It protects the work surface when perforating tools are being used, and may also double as an embossing pad.

Perforating Tools

For centuries, designs have been copied from one object to another by the pricking of paper. Today, a sewing wheel and carbon paper are still used to transfer a pattern on to fabric. Before the introduction of the sewing wheel, a needle tool would be used for the same purpose, and, around the sixteenth century, ground charcoal or chalk brushed through the holes would be used for transferring the pattern.

Wood-, tin-, lace- and leather-workers still use these techniques today.

For the purposes of parchment craft, a variety of needle tools are available, as follows:

- single-needle tool; perforates one hole at the time, but can also be used to emboss thin lines;

- double-needle tool; perforates two holes at a time, or one, if one needle is allowed to fall back into the last hole, which gives a more even result. This tool is used for pricking out round edges, but can also be used to emboss 'tramlines', either straight or wavy;

- four-needle tool; perforates a four-hole combination of 1mm square, which is used for decoration, or in the preparation for the cutting of crosses and slots.

All these tools are generally used to enhance parchment work with ornate decorations. It is of utmost importance to apply these tools at a dead vertical angle, in order to achieve round holes, and not to end up with oval-shaped ones.

Perforating Grid

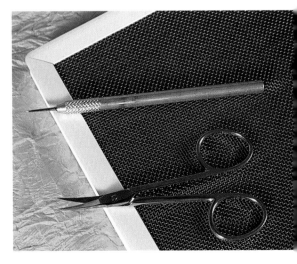

Most people use printed design sheets for marking the perforating grids by pricking through both parchment paper and design. Should you wish to do your own designing, this can be accomplished by using a perforating grid. The Kombi Grid is a wire-mesh grid with 1mm square holes. As it has a foam-rubber backing, it allows designing and embossing, as well as further perforating.

Adhesives

There are several types of glue available, including silicon glue, glue sticks, and paper or wood glues. The most important thing when using glues is to make sure that they are invisibly placed on to the card; do this by placing tiny blobs behind embossed, or painted, areas, or on the back page of a card right next to the spine, for example.

Inserts

To highlight work, or to prevent any text on the inside of a card being viewed through the front of the card, you can use an insert. This could be another piece of parchment paper, coloured paper, or rainbow paper.

To attach an insert to a card, you can either stitch it in, or you can perforate a couple of holes, thread a ribbon through the holes, and finish off with a bow.

Alternatively, you can glue the insert on to the card. Use UHU, the simplest, and most readily available, solution to most sticky problems. To avoid any ugly marks showing through the parchment paper, proceed as follows.

First, fold both the parchment card and the insert. Open both cards out, with the *open* side of the card in front of you. Gently squeeze the tube of UHU until a *tiny* blob of glue appears. Carefully affix this blob to the top of the fold line, then gently pull a thin gossamer of glue slightly away from the paper, towards the back page, and downwards,

towards the bottom of the fold line; here, adhere the end of this gossamer on to the paper. Fold the insert, line up its fold line with the fold line in the card, and adhere.

Stippling Tool

For perforating through the wire mesh from the perforating grid, it is advisable to use a tool with a thicker pin than the single-needle tool. This tool can also be used for stippling.

Parchment Scissors

To make the small cut crosses that are the hallmark of this craft, extremely fine pointed scissors are used. These are used to cut through the dams between the perforations, which are made using the four-needle tool.

If you have problems cutting the small holes, it may be easier to use lace patterns made with the Kombi Grid, as the holes are larger, and therefore the cutting with the small scissors is easier.

Perforations made with the single-needle, or two-needle tool, along borders, or in Richelieu-style patterns, can also be cut with these scissors. This will give a much nicer finish than removing the paper by 'tearing'.

Cutting a sheet of parchment paper

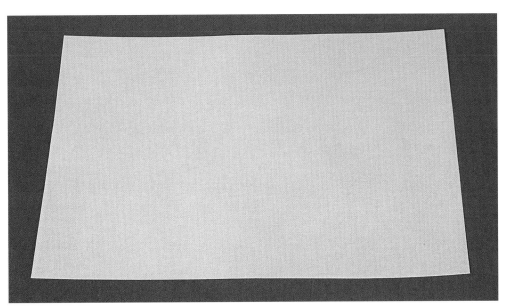

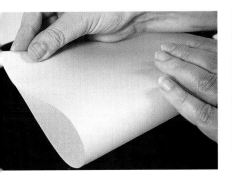 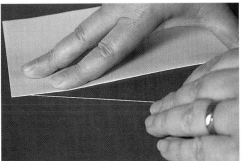 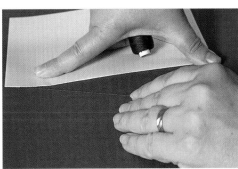

2 Let's Start Work

After reading through the Introduction and Chapter 1, and familiarizing yourself with the new words and terms, you can begin with a simple exercise. This will help you to get the hang of using the basic materials.

PROJECTS

Exercise 1

For this exercise you need:

- design no. 1
- sticky tape (low-tack)
- sheet of parchment paper (A4 = full size)
- mapping pen
- white ink for tracing
- medium ball embossing tool
- embossing pad
- glass of water, for cleaning pen
- kitchen paper

Design no. 1.

BEGINNING

Place the design on the table, but not on the embossing pad. Take two small pieces of low-tack sticky tape, fold each into three, with the sticky side out. Adhere these rolls of tape to the pattern sheet, but not on the design itself. Determine the rough side of the parchment paper, and affix the parchment to the pattern sheet, with the rough side uppermost.

TRACING

Give the bottle of ink a good shake. Dip the nib of the mapping pen into the ink, as far as the little hole in the centre; alternatively, if you have a plastic bottle with a nozzle, apply a drop of ink into the reservoir.

Trace the design very thinly; holding the pen as vertically as possible, you should merely 'float' over the paper. Trace every detail separately, without going back over the ink for a second time. Thicker and rougher lines will spoil the final result.

If you are not sure whether you have traced all of the design, carefully use a ruler to lift the parchment paper off the pattern, and check for any irregularities.

(At this stage you may decide to make this a practice sheet in four steps for future reference; trace the same design three more times on to the same sheet of parchment paper.)

Gently lift the parchment paper to remove it from the design, taking care not to fold it back sharply, as this will leave irreversible crease marks.

EMBOSSING

Turn the parchment paper over, ink side down, on to the softer side of the embossing pad.

(If you have decided to make this a sampler; do not emboss the first tracing but start with the first instruction on the second, third and fourth tracings. Continue with embossing, following steps 2 and 3, omitting every previous tracing.)

1. Using the medium embossing tool, trace over the outline of the

petals, the bottom half of the flower centres, some parts of the leaves, and the 'tramlines' of the surrounding stem.
2. Now trace over the whole of the design, including the dots, but *not* the fine lines of the stamens.

3. With the back of the embossing tool, gently rub over the leaves, on both sides of the vein.

Exercise 2

With this exercise, you can try some further embossing techniques, using the same pattern.

For this exercise you need:

◆ design no. 1 (page 17)

◆ sticky tape (low-tack)

◆ parchment paper

◆ mapping pen

◆ white ink for tracing

◆ medium ball embossing tool

◆ large ball embossing tool

◆ embossing pad

◆ single-needle tool

◆ glass of water, for cleaning pen

◆ kitchen paper

You can use this design to make a variety of cards. You could, for example, place the flower design in the centre, with a nice border design. A photocopier can reduce or enlarge the pattern according to your requirements.

SHADING

It is a good idea to try out some embossing on a spare piece of paper, to see what kind of embossing looks best. This is useful practice, and creates a lovely sampler for future reference.

A good way of learning to shade is by drawing or tracing a couple of petals. If you think you cannot draw petals, use heart shapes, which are very similar. Gently shade both petals in exactly the same way. Now use the second petal to do some more shading, applying the same *thickness* of lines but not necessarily *on* the same lines. You will find that the shading on the second petal gives more effect than the shading on the first.

All shading with the embossing tool follows the same principles:

1. With the large ball embossing tool, emboss from the traced line downwards towards the centre, but not along the whole length.
2. Emboss one petal at a time.
3. Keep the lines as close together as possible, and work in the direction of the veins.

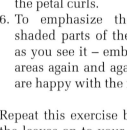

4. Embossing in uneven strokes – long strokes near the outlines, shorter strokes in between – will create an illusion of depth.

5. Some areas of the petals are more shaded – for example, where one petal overlaps another, or where the petal curls.

6. To emphasize the more shaded parts of the petal – as you see it – emboss these areas again and again, until you are happy with the result.

Repeat this exercise by tracing some of the leaves on to your sampler. With the large ball embossing tool, emboss each tip of the leaf in light strokes in a downward motion, towards the centre vein. Leaving a 'grey' area closest to the centre vein, and between each tip of the leaf, creates an illusion of depth.

Now trace the whole design. Emboss as before, but exclude the outlines of the flower petals.

Repeat all the embossing techniques you have learnt so far.

STIPPLING

This is a decorating/embossing technique that can give another dimension to your work.

Turn the embossing pad over, hard side uppermost, or work on a piece of board. Place the traced parchment paper upside down on this hard surface.

With the single-needle tool held at a vertical angle, stipple the flower centres, and between the 'tramlines' of the stem. Keep the pricking dense. The point of the needle should make tiny marks in the paper. When it is turned over, these marks will give a nice white-out effect on the front of the work.

Exercise 3 – Bookmark

This is an easy perforating exercise to follow your first attempt.

For this exercise you need:

◆ design no. 2

◆ sticky tape (low-tack)

Design no. 2.

◆ parchment paper, 100 × 200mm, white 150 gsm

◆ mapping pen

◆ white ink for tracing

◆ double-needle tool

◆ perforating mat

◆ medium ball embossing tool

◆ large ball embossing tool

◆ embossing pad

◆ glass of water, for cleaning pen

◆ kitchen paper

Attach the parchment paper, rough side uppermost to the pattern, using two pieces of folded sticky tape.

TRACING

Using the mapping pen and the white ink, trace the design thinly, avoiding 'over-tracing'.

Attaching and tracing the pattern:

1. *Roll sticky tape.*
2. *Affix sticky tape to pattern.*
3. *Place parchment on pattern.*
4. *& 5. Fill nib.*
6.–9. *Tracing the pattern.*

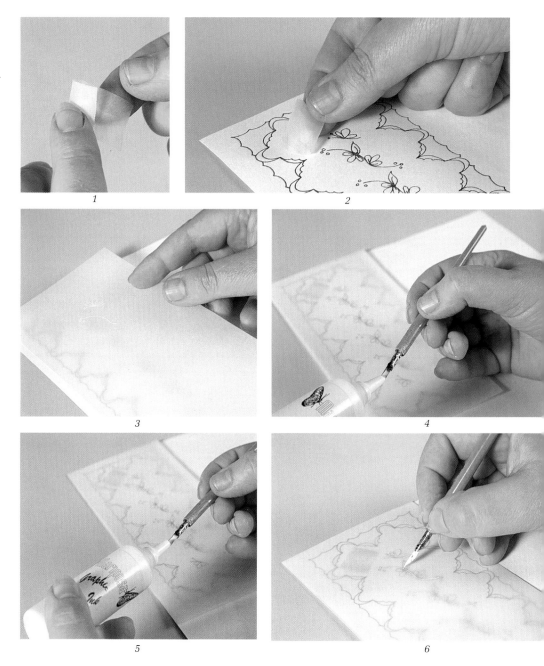

7

8

9

EMBOSSING

With the medium ball tool, gently emboss the border and the butterflies' wings.

When you emboss the dots, it is important to start in the centre, moving the embossing tool in a circular motion, gradually stretching the paper until it appears white.

Emboss the flower petals from the top downwards, but not all the way. Emboss the butterflies' wings from the body upwards, but not all the way. Emboss the leaves with the wrong end of the embossing tool. With the large ball tool, emboss the sickle shapes.

PERFORATING

Use the double-needle tool to perforate along the outside of the scalloped lines, using the full length of the needles. Let the first needle fall back into the last hole, as this gives a nice even spacing.

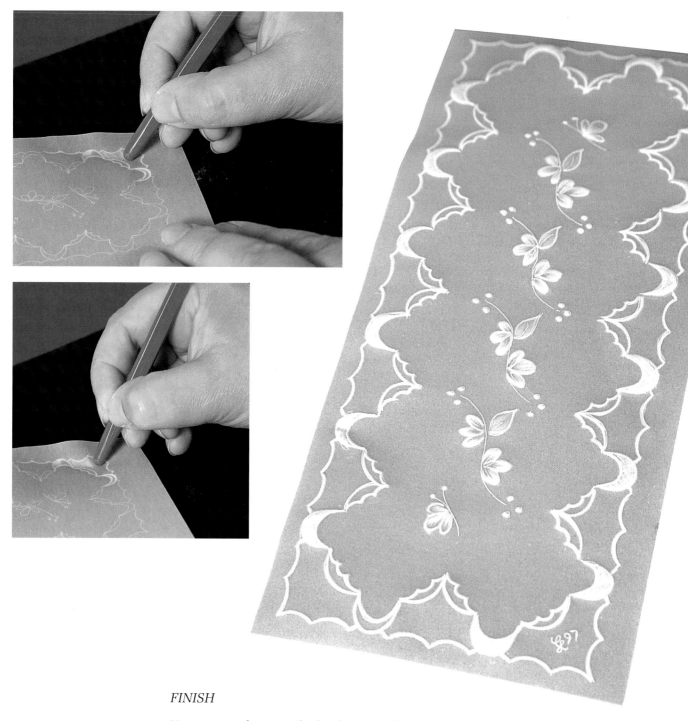

FINISH

You may wish to cut the bookmark with normal scissors alongside the perforations, to keep them as a decoration. Alternatively, you can press with the tip of a finger in front of the perforations; this will loosen the bookmark from its surrounding paper, and leave a lacy edge.

Exercise 4 – Summer Flowers in Semi-Oval

This exercise shows you how to accomplish a three-dimensional effect by using the different embossing techniques, including shading, which you have already practised.

You will notice that again the stems have not been embossed. This is to keep them as thin as possible and in the background. The most prominent parts are the flowers, the wheat and the seed heads.

For the leaves and the seed containers, use the wrong end of the embossing tool or, very lightly, the large ball tool.

Design no. 3.

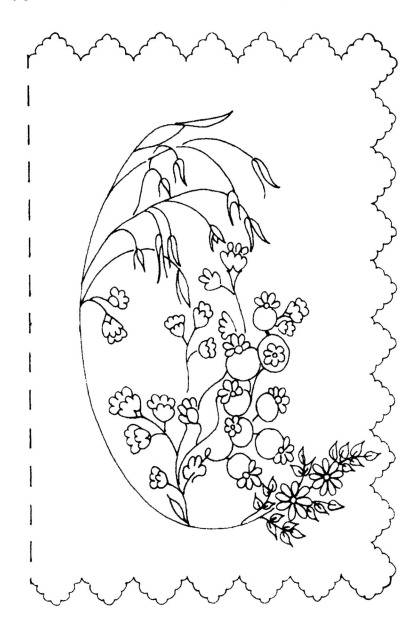

The illustration (*left*) shows how the areas are to be shaded.

For this exercise you need:

- design no. 3 (page 25)

- sticky tape (low-tack)

- parchment paper, 220 × 170mm, white 150 gsm

- mapping pen

- white ink for tracing

- double-needle tool

- perforating mat

- medium ball embossing tool

- large ball embossing tool

- embossing pad

- glass of water, for cleaning pen

- kitchen paper

Attach the parchment paper with the rough side uppermost on to the pattern, using two pieces of rolled sticky tape.

TRACING

With a white pencil and a ruler, trace the dashed fold line. Trace the rest of the design thinly with white ink. Carefully detach the parchment paper from the pattern.

EMBOSSING

With the medium ball tool, emboss the outlines of the seed containers, the semi-oval, the wheat, the flowers, the dots in the seed heads and the scalloped edge of the border.

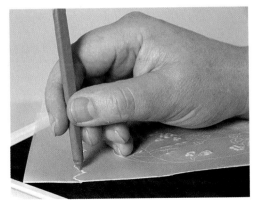

With the large ball tool, bring shading to the large leaf at the top, and emboss parts of the small leaves.

Use the wrong end of the embossing tool gently to emboss the seed containers.

PERFORATING

With the single-needle tool, perforate a hole in the centre of the dots in the seed heads. With the double-needle tool, perforate along the outside of the scalloped edge.

FINISH

Score the fold line using a ruler and the medium ball tool, and fold the card on this line. Carefully remove excess paper, loosening the paper by pressing with a fingertip just below the perforated edge.

ROSE MADDER
CRIMSON
COLD PINK
ROSE PINK
MAGENTA
GRAY ROSE
GRAY PINK
PALE
CHROME YELLOW
ORED
LIGHT BLUE
COBALT BLUE
PRUSSIAN BLUE
ULTRAMARINE DA
WARM GR
BEIGE

3 Further Steps

Once you are familiar with some of the basic techniques, you can begin to look at ways of enhancing your work. These could include using metallic or pearlescent inks, or oil pastels, to colour the parchment paper. Oil pastels, particularly, may be used in a number of different ways, including spot colouring, background colouring, colouring a whole sheet, and rainbow colouring.

METALLIC AND PEARLESCENT INKS

Metallic inks contain metallic particles in a base fluid. The particles have a habit of clogging at the bottom of the bottle, so these inks need to be shaken really well before use. Most ink bottles contain a small ball bearing to help to mix the particles with the base fluid.

To get the right results with these inks, use an old-fashioned steel nib, as this will give a slightly thicker line.

When you are tracing with white ink, you need to do it as thinly as possible. In contrast, with a metallic ink you need to trace more thickly and heavily, except when you are using it as a way of putting some of the final accents in place.

Use a plastic coffee stirrer to mix the ink after shaking the bottle thoroughly; also use the stirrer, or a cheap plastic child's paintbrush, to transfer ink on to the nib.

Be very careful not to overload your pen. This may result in the ink draining off the pen as soon as you place the nib

on to the parchment paper, spoiling your work. If you get a tiny blob of ink on your work (everyone does, from time to time), tear a piece of tissue paper, roll it up tightly, and use the rough edge to soak up the blob.

When the ink is dry, you can use an eraser or scalpel blade to remove any surplus.

Use pearlescent ink or diluted pearlescent paint for a shiny effect.

OIL PASTELS

Although parchment work looks attractive when it is left white, or with just a subtle addition of gold or silver, there are times when some colour can contribute enormously to the effect.

Spot Colouring

Oil pastel is generally applied before embossing begins, but, even after a card has been finished, for example, colour may be added.

Simply apply a little of the required colour on top of the already embossed work, then gently rub it with the tip of your finger to spread it. You can use artists' rolled-paper stumps to apply the colour to your work. Simply add some white spirit to the tip of the stump, apply your colour and transfer it on to the parchment.

Background Colour

To apply a background colour, prepare a folded piece of kitchen paper with a drop of white spirit, rub some oil pastel, in a contrasting colour, on to it, and apply this *around* the embossed area on the reverse side of the card.

Try not to rub any colour over already embossed areas on the reverse side, as this will influence the colour on the right side of the card.

Exercise 5 – Background Colour

For this exercise you need:

◆ oil pastels

◆ parchment paper

◆ board to protect work area

◆ low-tack sticky tape

◆ white spirit or odourless lighter fuel (solvent)

◆ kitchen paper

Applying a background colour (continued overleaf).

Applying a background colour (continued).

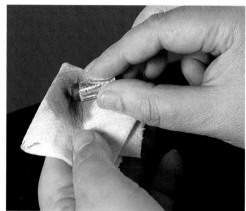

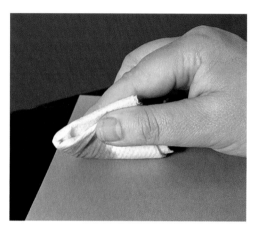

You should now have an evenly coloured sheet of parchment paper. When it is embossed on the side that you have coloured, the design will show in white on the reverse side of the paper – I like to call this the 'Wedgwood effect'.

If the paper is embossed on its non-coloured side, the design will show as a lighter shade of the colour on the coloured side of the paper.

Rainbow Colouring

You can colour a full A4 sheet of parchment paper as follows:

Stick the paper in place on a piece of board, using a piece of low-tack sticky tape at each corner.

To avoid lines and streaks, use a piece of kitchen paper folded in four, then doubled. Add some solvent (white spirit or lighter fuel) to the kitchen paper, then apply enough oil pastel, and spread this over the parchment paper; apply more colour if needed.

Take a clean piece of kitchen paper, fold it, and wipe it evenly over the full length of the paper to remove any superfluous oil pastel; this will also dry off any excess solvent.

The application of alternate colours to parchment paper, either in straight lines, in a circle or in semi-circles, can give a totally new dimension to your work. The technique is much the same as colouring a sheet of paper all in one colour, but this time you finish one stripe of colour before applying the next, blending each successive colour with the last one for the best effect.

Blot off any excess solvent by placing a full sheet of kitchen paper over the worked area, and patting carefully all over. Use another clean piece of kitchen paper to remove any surplus residue.

Keep a sheet of kitchen paper at hand to protect your work from smearing, and to wipe your hands when you have

finished applying the oil pastel. While the paper is wet you must not touch any worked areas, as this is likely to leave fingerprints. If you are not happy with the result, simply apply white spirit to a piece of kitchen paper, wipe the whole thing clean, and try again.

Marbled Colouring

Another effective way to show off white work is marbling. This is done by placing large dots of oil pastel on to a sheet of parchment paper, in matching colours, such as pink and purple, green and orange, red and blue. You can also use more than two colours if you like – have a go with different combinations. If you don't like it, clean it, using a sheet of kitchen paper and white spirit. Dry the paper off before your next attempt.

Special Effects

You can achieve special effects – lines, squares, horizontal cross-hatchings, or diagonal cross-hatchings – by masking off areas with strips of low-tack sticky tape.

A die-cut shape – heart, round, oval, or square – placed over an existing piece of work can make a nice frame when the area around it is coloured with oil pastels.

If you have been practising, and have come up with a masterpiece, use this technique to make your 'doodle' into a card. Simply cover the work with a piece of card with a cut-out shape that suits the design, and give the surrounding area an appropriate colour.

Exercise 6 – Best Wishes Envelope Card

In addition to all the equipment you have used so far, you will need:

- ◆ design no. 4

- ◆ parchment paper, 170 × 225mm, white 150 gsm

- ◆ fine stylus embossing tool

- ◆ gold ink, or pearlescent ink

- ◆ steel-nib pen for metallic ink

- ◆ paper kitchen towel

- ◆ oil pastel (turquoise was used in this example)

Design no. 4.

- white spirit or odourless lighter fuel (solvent)

- white pencil and ruler

TRACING AND COLOURING

Attach the parchment paper, with the rough side uppermost, to your pattern, using two rolled pieces of low-tack sticky tape.

Trace the fold line with white pencil. Using white ink, trace the daffodil trumpet and its four connecting petals.

With gold ink, trace the stamens and the rest of the design. When using the steel-nib pen for the metallic ink, you do not need to apply too much pressure, as the ink will flow easily down the nib. Remember also that metallic ink needs more time to dry.

When the ink is dry, gently detach the parchment paper from the pattern and turn the paper over, with the ink side down.

On the smooth side, colour the whole sheet of parchment paper (*see* page 32).

EMBOSSING

On the smooth side, using the fine stylus embossing tool, emboss the design that has been traced.

With the medium ball tool, emboss the folded parts of the large leaves, the top of the trumpet, the connecting petals, and *alongside* the gold embossed lines.

With the large ball tool, emboss *between* the lines of the triangular shapes. Draw the fine lines in the outer border, using the double-needle tool. (Hold the tool at a horizontal slant.)

PERFORATING

With the double-needle tool, perforate *round* the scalloped flap of the envelope (*see* illustration). Leave the flap connected to the envelope, as this looks neater.

Score and fold the card.

Using the double-needle tool, perforate through both layers, *round* the outer edge. Discard waste paper.

Exercise 7 – Art Nouveau Heart

This design has a lot of detail and gives you more of a challenge. It could be used for many occasions, Valentines Day springs to mind, but also Mothering Sunday. I trust you will find a suitable occasion. If you find the size of the card too large, reduce it on a photocopier to meet your requirements.

For this exercise you need:

- design no. 5

- parchment paper; size 260mm × 200mm, white 150 gsm

- mapping pen for white ink

- white ink

- silver ink, or pearlescent ink

- steel-nib pen for metallic ink

- glass of water

- medium ball embossing tool, and embossing pad

- stippling tool

- double-needle tool, and perforating pad

- oil pastels: fuchsia, skin colour and green, or your taste

- board, to protect work area

- low-tack sticky tape

- white spirit, or odourless lighter fuel (solvent)

- paper kitchen towel

- white pencil and ruler

Attach the parchment paper with the rough side uppermost, using two pieces of rolled, low-tack, sticky tape onto the pattern. Trace the fold line with white pencil.

Design no. 5.

TRACING

Use white ink to trace all the flowers, leaves, berries, and the border. Trace with silver ink the rest of the design.

Remove the parchment paper from the pattern, turn over, and place with the smooth side uppermost on the board.

OIL PASTELS

Use the fuchsia oil pastel to colour the large scrolls, skin colour behind the large flowers and dotted around, green amongst all the other colours.

Fold a sheet of paper towel first in eight, and then roll this into a pencil shape. Add a tiny amount of the solvent, and use this to spread the colours evenly, starting with the scrolls and the flowers.

With a clean part of the paper towel gently mix the other colours, resembling marble.

Transfer the parchment paper, with the coloured side uppermost, onto the embossing pad.

EMBOSSING

From the back: with the medium ball tool emboss all the flower petals, the berries, and the heart shape; with the large ball, tool the leaves.

Turn the paper over, smooth side uppermost; highlight the scroll with the large ball tool or use the 'wrong end' of the embossing tool.

STIPPLING

Using the stippling tool, work the spaces between the scrolls.

FINISH

Score and fold the card. Using the double-needle tool, perforate through both layers round the outer edge. Discard waste paper.

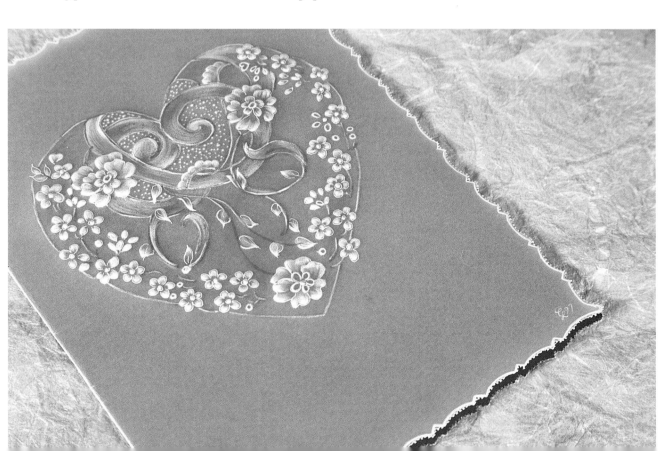

CUTTING

Cutting is the technique that gives parchment craft its distinctive look. When you start to use scissors to cut between the perforations, instead of using your fingertips to 'tear' the paper, your lacework will be transformed.

The cutting technique is not as difficult as it looks. It gives a much neater result, and the basics of the technique will be excellent preparation for when you come to cut four-hole combinations into little crosses. These crosses are one of the features for which parchment craft is so admired.

The Scissors

There are many different qualities of scissors available, with the relevant variety in prices. Look for scissors with minute points, so that you can insert the very tips into the perforations, without pushing or tearing.

The ends of the blades should be slightly rounded – rather like the shape of a fingernail – and not straight. Rounded blades will not only help to keep the holes visible, when the points enter, but they also give the best cut.

TIP:

A little beeswax or candle wax on the tips of the scissors makes cutting easier.

Holding the Scissors

This seems a strange way of holding the scissors, but if you try to cut holding the scissors in the traditional way, you will soon feel the strain. Hold the scissors as follows:

1. place the scissors on the table, points down;
2. insert the index finger and the middle finger in the holes, and pull the scissors towards the table edge;
3. now place your thumb underneath both fingertips and lift the scissors off the table;
4. replace your thumb towards the side of the index finger, but still on the scissors for support. Practise this a few times, until you feel quite comfortable with the scissors.

Preparation

Before cutting four-hole combinations, you need to prepare the perforations.

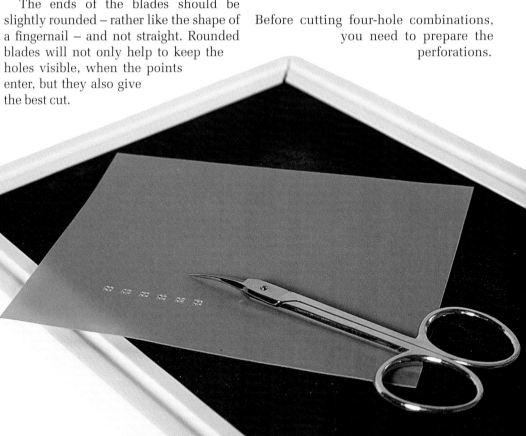

In order to achieve the best results, you will need to perforate twice. First, mark the area, by perforating without using the whole length of the needles. If you plan to do any embossing in the same area, do this next. After finishing the embossing, you will need to re-perforate, this time letting the needles use their full length. As long as you have kept your perforating tool in the upright position, the holes will be nice and round.

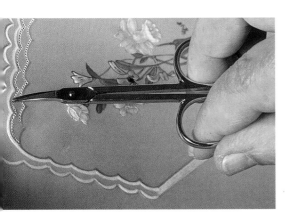

Cutting along a Row of Perforations

Pick up the scissors. If you are right-handed, hold the parchment paper with your left hand.

Insert the very tips of the points of the scissors into the first two holes.

At this point, hold the scissors slightly downwards, pushing the 'dam' of paper between the holes a little upwards.

Now, twist the scissors slightly to the left, and clip. You should hear the paper make a clicking sound.

Put the right blade point back in the last cut, and the left blade point in the next hole. Repeat this procedure until you have finished cutting.

If you are left-handed, reverse the operation, holding the paper in the right hand. Start cutting from the left-hand side, put the left blade point back in the last cut, and the right blade point in the following hole.

Use this technique not only for borders, but also for small perforated areas where pieces of paper need to be taken out.

Cutting Crosses

As with cutting along a row of perforations, when you cut crosses, you will need to line up the scissors *beneath* the holes. As long as you remember this,

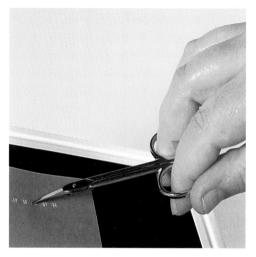

you cannot go wrong. Whatever you do, keep the scissors *below* the set of perforations you are about to cut.

The only difference with cutting crosses is that you need to *turn* the paper around, and you work from the *inside* of the four-hole perforations. Each cross consists of four turns.

If you want to cheat, cut the top two holes and then the bottom two holes first, then turn and repeat this procedure with the remaining two sets of two-hole perforations. The result will be an odd-looking hole!

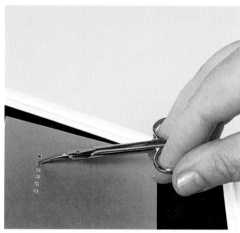

Cutting a Slot

Cut all of the dams between the perforations along the top row, turn the paper round one-quarter of the design, and cut. Turn the design again and cut along the top row of the perforations, then turn a last time and cut the remaining perforations.

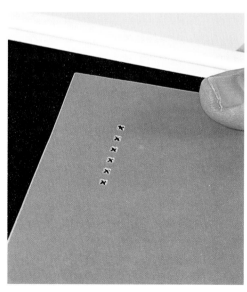

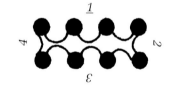

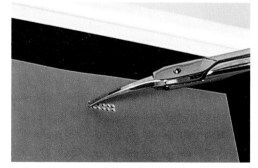

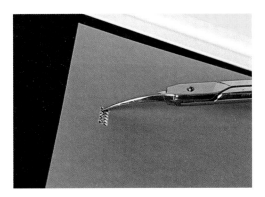

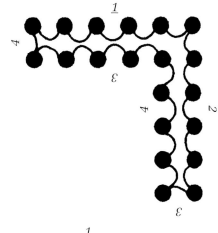

Saving Time

If you have a lot of cutting to do, you can save time by cutting along all the top perforations first, then turning, and so on. When cutting large pieces, I work like this, but finish each pattern individually.

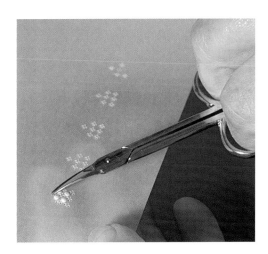

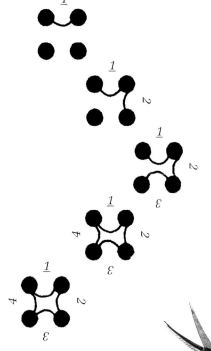

Exercise 8 – Open Lace Card

As well as the usual equipment, for this perforating exercise you will need:

- design no. 6 (page 42)

- parchment paper, 180 × 160mm, white 150 gsm

Attach the parchment paper to the pattern, using two small rolled pieces of low-tack sticky tape, with the rough side of the parchment paper uppermost.

TRACING

Trace the whole design with gold ink. Do not trace the dots of the perforating grid. Thinly draw the fold line with a white pencil and ruler.

Design no. 6.

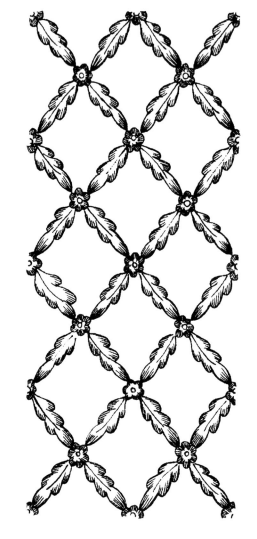

EMBOSSING

With the small ball tool, emboss lightly the tips of the petals. Begin at the top of the petal, and work along one side first, then towards the other side. Emboss the front (heaviest) part of the petals slightly whiter than the back. With the same tool, emboss the leaves, again starting at the tip of the leaf, and working each leaf separately.

Use the extra-small ball tool to emboss six small dots as stamens in the little flowers in the lattice.

The area between the tramlines is embossed with the large ball tool.

PERFORATING

Use the double-needle tool to perforate the paper, following the perforating grid. Be as precise as possible; taking care to perforate *outside* the gold ink, not *on* it, as this would spoil the design.

CUTTING

With the fine parchment scissors, cut the dams between the perforations. Carefully remove all superfluous paper, leaving a lovely open lattice to be proud of.

FINISH

Score the fold line along a ruler with the extra-small ball tool. Fold the card. Insert a piece of rainbow paper in the colours of your choice. Cut out round the outer edge.

TIP:

An insert of parchment paper with a flower design, or message, showing through the lattice, or maybe a butterfly or dragonfly attached to the front, could add another dimension to this card.

Exercise 9 – Open Border Card

As well as the usual equipment, for this cutting exercise you will need:

◆ design no. 7

◆ parchment paper

Design no. 7.

Attach the parchment paper to the pattern in the usual way with low-tack sticky tape, rough side uppermost.

TRACING

For the front page, trace the shapes surrounding the small flowers with white ink. Use gold ink for the scallops, and the two small designs in the corners.

Trace the fold line and outer edge with white pencil. Detach the parchment paper from the pattern, and turn over. The inked side is face down.

Re-align the traced fold line and outer lines with the lines on the pattern. The front page should now be on the left-hand side of the fold line, facing down.

With the gold ink, trace the small petals and dots. Let this dry completely, allowing the gold ink a little longer to dry than white ink.

Detach the parchment paper from the pattern and turn the paper over, with the small flowers facing down. Apply strips of low-tack sticky tape on either side of the border, to mask off the centre of the card and the outer edge.

OIL PASTEL

Draw stripes of oil pastel (blue was used here) inside the tramlines of the protecting strips of sticky tape. Spread this with a folded piece of kitchen paper and a little white spirit. Remove any excess moisture with a dry piece of kitchen paper, before carefully removing the sticky tape from the parchment paper.

EMBOSSING

With the medium ball tool, emboss all of the white tracing. Use the extra-small ball tool to emboss inside the gold petals and the small dots.

CUTTING

With the fine parchment scissors, cut the dams between the perforations. Remove waste paper.

FINISH

Score the fold line along a ruler with the medium ball tool. Fold the card, making sure that the holes in the front page cover the flowers on the back page.

Cut out along the pencil line.

Exercise 10 – Easter Card

As well as the usual equipment, for this crosses-cutting exercise you will need:

◆ design no. 8

◆ parchment paper, 120 × 220mm, white 150 gsm

Design no. 8.

The stars in the centres of the petals are embossed with the star tool. Alternatively, you can emboss a large dot, or stipple five dots in a circle with a stippling tool or single-needle tool.

PERFORATING

Use the double-needle tool to perforate the border, as indicated.

Applying oil pastels.

Attach the parchment paper to the pattern with rolled-up low-tack sticky tape, rough side uppermost.

TRACING

Trace the fold line with white pencil. Trace the flower petals with white ink. Using sepia ink, trace the leaves, the stems, the flower centres, and the stamens. The words can be traced with metallic or pearlescent ink.

OIL PASTELS

Working on the front of the paper, apply a little green inside the leaves. Spread it carefully with a rolled paper stump.

Use yellow for the petals and orange for the centres. Detach the parchment from the patterns and turn over, smooth side uppermost.

Apply blue oil pastel to the top half of the design, and yellow to the lower half. With a folded piece of kitchen towel, and some white spirit, gently smooth the blue colour first, then the yellow. Now blend the two colours along the middle.

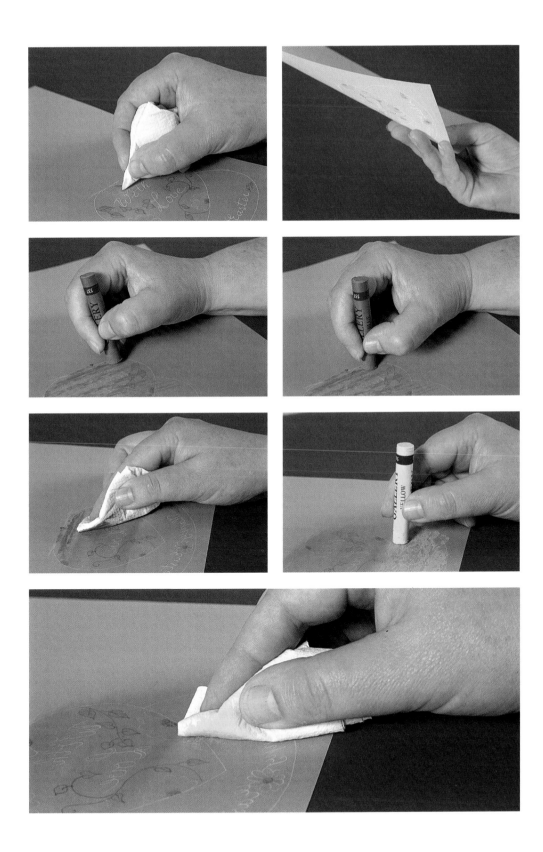

EMBOSSING – 1

From the front, using the single-needle tool, draw a fine line in the centre of the petals, beginning at the top. Turn the paper over.

With the medium ball tool, emboss the outlines of the heart shape and the egg shape. Emboss the petals, starting at one side of the petal, gradually moving along to the other side. Do not emboss the whole length of the petals, but give depth to the flower; remember the principles of shading. With the wrong end of an embossing tool, shade only part of the leaves.

For the little stars along the border there is a special tool, which can be obtained from specialist craft shops. Alternatively, trace the grid in white ink and emboss this from the back with the fine stylus.

STIPPLING

Stipple the centres of the flowers using the single-needle tool.

PERFORATING – 1ST STAGE

Re-attach the parchment paper to the pattern and gently pre-perforate the centre design with the four-needle tool, as per the grid.

EMBOSSING – 2

With the fine stylus and a ruler, emboss the double lines between the perforations.

PERFORATING – 2ND STAGE

To make cutting much easier, and neater, cut only a cross in the centre of the grids, and re-perforate only the centre four-hole combinations of the grid perforations.

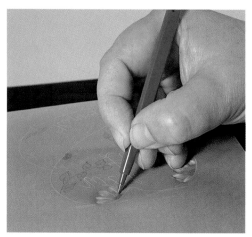

CUTTING

With the fine parchment scissors, using the diagram as a guide, cut the centre four-hole perforations to crosses.

FINISH

Score the fold line, using the fine stylus and a ruler. With the two-needle tool, perforate, scallop-wise, around the little stars, through both layers of the folded card. Leave, as a hinge, two connecting areas at the top of the card. Cut the dams between the perforations, and discard the excess paper.

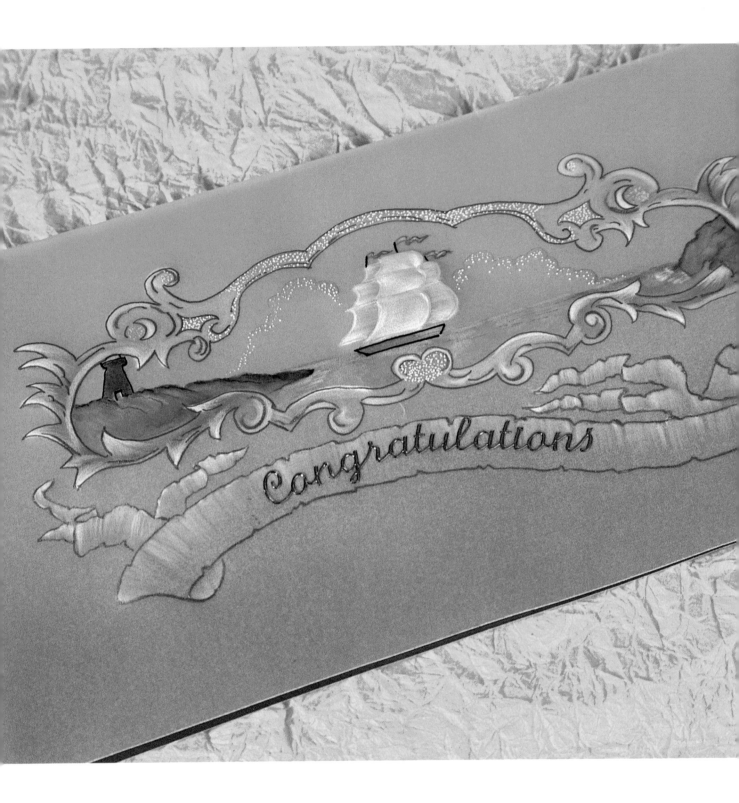

Congratulations

4 Painting with Felt-tip Pens

Using felt-tip pens for painting on parchment paper is a rather modern approach to the craft.

This technique can be used in various ways. The colours are strongest when applied neat, but they may also be worked with a brush, to give a softer, shaded appearance.

When the ink is applied neat on the reverse side of the paper, the colour changes to a toned-down version, when viewed from the front.

PAINTING WITH A BRUSH

In order to prepare for painting with inks, it is a good idea to learn first how to work with the highly useful medium of felt-tip pen ink. You should get the hang of working with the brush – using the *line* and *scrub* techniques – much more quickly than if you were to start using inks or paints straight away.

Learning to paint with felt-tip pen ink is a useful exercise, for the following reason. When you paint on parchment paper, which does not absorb very well, the pigment level of the medium used should be as low as possible. The pigment level in most inks is too high for use on parchment paper, so a fair amount of water is needed to thin the ink. It is difficult to get this dilution exactly right, and, if your brush is too wet, and you use the ink 'as it comes', ugly water marks will appear once the ink is dry. When

you use felt-tip pen ink with a brush, only a little ink is dispensed, and there is no risk of over-wetting.

The consistency of the ink in the felt-tip pen is much the same as that of the inks that you have so far only used for tracing. Water-based felt-tip pens are used because the ink from these pens takes a long time to dry when used on parchment paper, giving ample time to work with the damp brush. Do not attempt to use spirit-based felt-tip pens. These dry much too quickly, and leave strong pigment lines, which will spoil your work.

You will need a sable-hair brush No.2, and good-quality, water-based felt-tip pens. A sable-hair brush will retain water, and the brush will stay dampened, unlike a synthetic brush.

Start with just one colour, for example, green for leaves. This will give you a good indication of how much ink is required.

Painting Leaves – The Line Technique

1. Trace some small leaves in sepia or green ink.
2. Dampen a No.2 brush with some water; take off any excess water by dabbing on a clean piece of kitchen paper.
3. Draw a stripe of green felt-tip ink inside the leaf.

4. With the tip of the brush, move the ink lengthwise, in vertical zigzag lines, taking the ink across the leaf from one side to the other.

5. To paint a vein, repeat step 4, to half-way across the leaf.

6. Stay on the vein and keep mov-ing the brush, until a darker line appears.

7. Try this technique also on some larger leaves. For a larger area, the brush needs to be slightly wetter.

Exercise 11 – Flowers

As well as the usual equipment, for this felt-tip exercise you will need:

◆ design no. 9

◆ parchment paper, 250 × 170mm

After some trial runs with the felt-tip pen and brush on a spare piece of parchment paper, you should feel confident enough to try this design.

Adhere the parchment paper to the pattern in the usual way.

TRACING

Trace the fold line with white pencil. With sepia ink and using the mapping pen, trace the whole design. Detach the parchment paper from the pattern and turn the paper over.

PAINTING

On the reverse side, apply a stripe of light green felt-tip pen, just inside the outline, on one of the leaves.

Spread the paint with a damp brush from one side to the other. Take care not to leave too much ink at the end, as this may cause bubbling of the paper.

Repeat this on the other leaves.

With a mixture of skin colour and fuchsia, paint the flower petals in the same way.

The leaves in the border are coloured with a dark green felt-tip pen; again, spread the ink with the brush.

Design no. 9.

Use a yellow felt-tip pen for the stem of the top flower, and brown for the other stems. Do not brush these, as you need a stronger colour for the stems.

Wait until the ink is completely dry before turning the paper over, to face the front. Now add some fuchsia felt-tip colour to the centres and stamens of the flowers, and let this dry.

EMBOSSING

With the large ball tool, emboss the flower petals from the front of the paper; the cupped centres and leaves are embossed from the back.

STIPPLING

With the single-needle tool, using the back of the embossing pad, or a piece of board, stipple the scallops inside the oval, the stamens, and underneath the border leaves.

Using a ruler, draw cross-hatch decorations in the border.

FINISH

Score and fold the paper. Use plain or fancy scissors to cut round the edge.

TIP:

This card also looks good traced with white ink, and using oil pastels.

Painting Petals – The Line Technique

1. Trace some flowers in a colour of your choice.
2. Draw a stripe of felt-tip pen ink on the inside of the petal.
3. With the tip of a damp No.2 brush, move the ink to the other side of the petal.
4. Repeat step 3 on the following petal, and so on.

Painting Petals – The Scrub Technique

TIP:

Dampen the brush *before* application of the felt-tip pen ink. The felt-tip pen ink must not be allowed to dry before the brush is applied to the paper.

Check the illustrations for guidance on colours and embossing.

1. Trace some petals in a colour of your choice.
2. Draw a stripe of felt-tip pen ink just below the top of the petal.
3. Place the tip of a damp No.2 brush on the wet ink.
4. Making circular movements, and gradually pressing down the brush (as far as the pattern lets you), paint the petal from one side towards the other.
5. Still continuing the circular movements, gently lift the brush to its tip as the area to paint becomes smaller. Lift it off completely at the end, without going back.

Two-Colour Painting

Try this sampler; using the large flower design from the dragonfly card. The method is quite simple, as follows.

Draw two stripes of matching colours, for example, fuchsia and purple (*see* illustration).

With a clean damp brush, use the scrub technique to blend the two colours, as you paint from one side of the petal to the other side. Take care not to go in reverse, as this will spoil the work.

Exercise 12 – Large Flower, Best Wishes

As well as the usual equipment, for this felt-tip pen exercise you will need:

◆ design no. 10

◆ parchment paper, 190 × 250mm, white 150 gsm

◆ colours used: blue, turquoise

Attach the parchment paper to the pattern in the usual way.

TRACING

With white pencil, trace the fold line, and the tramlines of the outer border. Use gold ink and the steel-nib pen for the rest of the design.

FELT-TIP PEN AND BRUSH

Take the parchment paper off the design and turn it over, with the ink side down.

Design no. 10.

Start with the large flower in the centre. Using the turquoise felt-tip pen, draw a thin line just below the outer edge of one petal. With a damp brush, using the scrub technique, paint the petal, gradually going from one side to the other.

Although the petal is rather large, do not be deterred; press the hairs of the brush down, as far as the pattern will let you. Most of the colour will be on the upper two-thirds of the petal, leaving the area around the stamen white. Now colour the centre of the flower, and the curled lips of the petals, with neat turquoise ink from the felt-tip pen, without using the brush.

For the rest of the design, use a mixture of blue and turquoise. Paint a couple of the leaves as follows: apply a thin line of blue on the outer edge of the leaf, and with a damp No.2 brush, using the scrub technique, spread the ink from the base of the leaf to the tip. Then apply a thin line of turquoise on the outer edge of the leaf and, without cleaning the brush first, paint that side of the leaf from the base to the tip. To get a stronger turquoise colour, start with this colour first, and then apply the blue colour. The turned lips of the leaf and petal are coloured with neat blue, without using the brush.

If you play with the colours, you will find that you can create beautiful effects; they are much like the colour mixes you see in silk painting, which can be a wonderful inspiration.

EMBOSSING

Ensure the colours applied are completely dry before you begin embossing.

From the front, using the large ball tool, gently emboss inside the corners of the turned edges of the large central flower. Using the fine stylus, emboss all the petals, starting just below the outer edge. Remember to apply 'movement'. On these petals you can easily define the veins by making use of the shape of the scalloped contours. Take care not to emboss too sharply – build it up gradually and use the large ball tool, or the wrong end of your embossing tool, either to emphasize or tone down.

Remember that this work is all part of the exercise. If you are not sure you are doing it correctly, practise the shading technique on a spare piece of paper, using a black leaded pencil.

With the extra-small ball tool, emphasize some of the gold tracings of the flowers and leaves, to give movement, and emboss the lines of the outer border.

STIPPLING

Place the paper on a perforating pad, and, from the front, pierce in a random manner between the tramlines of the inner border using the stippling tool.

Alternatively, you may wish to use the perforating grid; line up the lines in the grid with the contours of the border, to give a more patterned effect.

FINISH

Score and fold the card. Use a text sticker if you wish to embellish your card with a greeting, or leave it blank. Trim the card, if necessary.

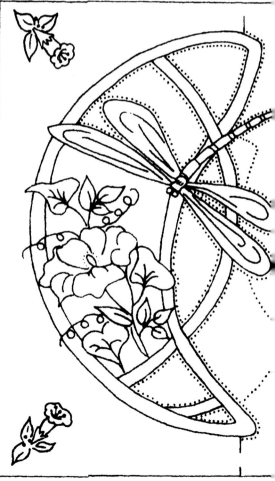

Exercise 13 – Art Nouveau Dragonfly and Butterfly

As well as the usual equipment, for this felt-tip pen exercise you will need:

- design no. 11

- parchment paper, 300 × 150mm, white 150 gsm

- colours used: butterfly – yellow, brown; dragonfly – green, turquoise; flower – skin, blue; leaves – mixed greens

Attach the parchment paper to the pattern in the usual way.

TRACING

With white pencil trace the outer border and fold lines. Use white ink for the tiny flowers in the corner decorations, and the flower petals in the butterfly section. With sepia ink trace the dragonfly, the large flower, the butterfly, the centres in the small flowers, and the rest of the corner decorations.

Use green ink for the leaves, stems and tendrils in the dragonfly section, and the leaves and stems in the butterfly section.

Design no. 11.

With gold ink, and using the steel-nib pen, trace the tramlines. Do not trace any of the small dots, which denote perforations, along the tramlines.

FELT-TIP PEN AND BRUSH

Work on the front of the paper.

For the dragonfly: apply a small dot of blue in the corners of the wings, and a thin stripe of turquoise in the centres. With a slightly damp brush, use the scrub technique. Starting at the outer tip of the wing, paint with the tip of the brush along the upper line of the wing – with the rest of the brush pushed down as far as the design will let you – towards the body. Gently lift the brush off. Turn the paper round, repeat the same work on the other half of the wing, and on the remaining wings.

Apply a thin stripe of light green to one side of the body; using the scrub technique, starting at the head, spread the colour to the end of the body. Do this by placing the tip of the brush against the upper outer edge and making small circular movements; take care not to let the brush protrude at the bottom outer edge.

Place tiny dots of neat blue on the eyes.

For the large flower: apply a thin line of blue along the outer edges of the petals, and the cupped shape at the base. Add a little skin colour, just below the blue line. With a damp brush, using the scrub technique, with the tip of the brush against the outer edge, and the bottom of the brush towards the centre of the flower, paint each petal shape separately. Paint the cup shape, and add a small dot of neat skin colour to the stamen.

Use the same colours for the small corner flowers.

For the butterfly: apply a thin line of brown along the outer rim of the wings, followed by a small stripe of red, and a larger area of yellow. With a damp brush, using the scrub technique, starting nearest the body, with the tip of the brush against the outline, paint towards the tip of the wing. Make your circular movements smaller and smaller, until you can gently lift the brush off. Replace the brush and repeat, painting towards the bottom corner of the wing; repeat the same procedure, and then follow on, painting towards the body. You should find that you now have a darker outline on the wings, and a lighter area nearer the body.

For the body: apply a thin line of brown along the outer edges and a small stripe of yellow in between. Gently spread the colour along one side of the body, starting at the head, down towards the end of the body. Use neat brown for the dots in the wings, and for the tiny dots on the feelers.

For the small leaves: apply a tiny dot of light green to all the small leaves. Spread the colour with the very tip of a damp brush.

For the large leaves: on the reverse side of the paper, apply a small stripe of dark green, plus a tiny dot of brown to the leaves. Paint with a damp brush from the outside of the leaf towards the centre vein, leaving a darker line by repeated brushing in that same area.

For the small flowers in the butterfly section: apply a tiny dot of neat yellow in the centres. Leave until completely dry.

OIL PASTEL

On the reverse side of the paper, apply a colour behind the main shape, using a folded piece of paper kitchen towel and a drop of white spirit. I used turquoise, but you may use any colour you choose.

EMBOSSING

All the embossing is done from the back.

Using the fine stylus tool, delicately emboss the dragonfly wings. With the extra-small ball tool, emboss the veins in the butterfly wings, the small flower petals, the stamen of the large flower, and the centre of the small flower. Emboss with the medium ball tool the large flower, the dots in the wings of the butterfly, and the butterfly body.

Use the large ball tool to smooth the dragonfly wings and those of the butterfly.

With the wrong end of the embossing tool, pre-stretch the area between the tramlines. Follow the same area with the metal ball end of the tool, and finish by filling in any remaining grey areas, using the medium ball tool.

PERFORATING

Using the double-needle tool, perforate along the dotted lines of the dragonfly section.

CUTTING

With the fine parchment scissors, cut between the dams of the perforations and remove the paper.

FINISH

Score the centre fold line, from the front of the paper, and from the back the small fold lines of the dragonfly section, using the extra-small ball tool and a ruler.

Fold the card along the centre line, so that the picture remains on the inside of the card. Gently fold the front page back on the small fold lines, simultaneously easing out the dragonfly's wings and body.

Using gold ink and the mapping pen, embellish the dragonfly wings, the flowers and some of the leaves, with gossamer-thin lines.

Exercise 14 – Ship in Art Nouveau Frame, Congratulations

As well as the usual equipment, for this felt-tip pen and brush exercise you will need:

◆ design no. 12 (page 60)

◆ parchment paper, 240 × 210mm, white 150 gsm

Design no. 12.

◆ colours used: for the dunes – brown, green, yellow; for the lighthouse, ship and flags – brown, yellow

TRACING

Trace the fold line with white pencil. With white pearlescent ink, trace the sails and the horizon. Use sepia ink for the dunes and flags, and black ink for the ship's hull and the flag poles.

Trace the frame surrounding the picture with blue pearlescent ink, and the banner and message (optional) with gold ink, using the steel-nib pen. Endorse some of the scrolls in the banner, and thinly trace the clouds with gold ink; use the mapping pen for this finer work.

FELT-TIP PEN AND BRUSH

Working from the front; apply neat yellow to the

flags, the window, and the door of the lighthouse.

For the ship, draw a stripe of brown on the left-hand side of the ship's hull, and a little yellow in the right-hand corner. Drag the brown into the yellow by placing the tip of a damp brush against the top of the hull, starting in the left-

For the sails: start on the outer embossed lines, emboss in horizontal lines towards the centre, leaving a greyish area in the centre of the middle sails. For the outer sails, emboss towards the middle sails. Using the medium ball tool, emboss the turret of the lighthouse and some shading in the frame surrounding the picture, accentuating the pointed waves.

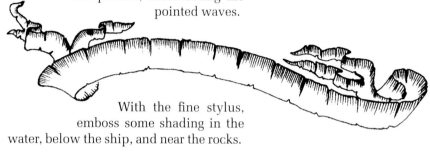

With the fine stylus, emboss some shading in the water, below the ship, and near the rocks.

STIPPLING

Place the parchment paper face down on to a piece of board. Stipple the central area at the top of the surrounding frame and the diamond shapes, the area just below the clouds, and the heart shape at the bottom of the frame.

FINISH

Score and fold the card.

hand corner and dragging along to the other side. Try to achieve the effect of an old wooden ship.

For the dunes: along the top of the dunes apply a thin line of green, followed by a thin line of yellow, and a larger area of brown.

EMBOSSING

With the extra-small ball tool, emboss the outlines of the sails and inside the flag. Use the large ball tool to emboss the shading in the banner.

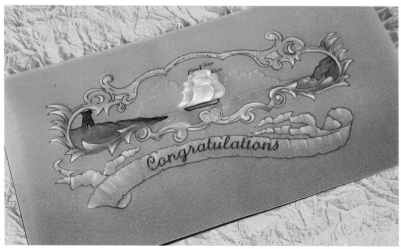

MIXING COLOURS

How do three colours make nine? The basic – or primary – colours are red, blue and yellow. Mixing two of these colours together results in the creation of secondary colours, as follows:

Red and blue = purple
Red and yellow = orange
Blue and yellow = green

These six colours can be mixed again to make other colours, called tertiary colours, as follows:

Red and green = brown
Brown and blue = grey
Brown and grey = black (almost)

Colour Exercise

Draw a Circle.
Draw one blue stripe, one yellow, one red, and then one more blue stripe, leaving a space between each of the colours.
With a wet No.2 brush, wash one-third of each colour over the clean space into the next colour, to make green, orange and purple.

Exercise 15 – Art Nouveau Paperweight

The paperweight is 550mm diameter, on the inside of the aperture.
As well as the usual equipment, for this felt-tip pen exercise you will need:

◆ design no. 13

◆ parchment paper, 65 × 65mm, white 150 gsm

Design no. 13.

TRACING

Attach the parchment paper to the pattern. With black ink, trace the whole design.

Exercise 16 – Shepherd With Flowers

As well as the usual equipment, for this felt-tip pen and crosses-cutting exercise you will need:

 ◈ design no. 14

Design no. 14.

FELT-TIP PEN

Work from the back. Use dark green for the large centre leaves; brown for the space between the large leaves; light green and a little orange for the flowers, and the small leaves beside the flowers; orange for the double spaces in the rim; and blue for the remaining areas.

EMBOSSING

Work from the back. With the extra-small ball tool, emboss the tips of the three upper petals, then the three little petal shapes in the centres, followed by the upper part of the two bottom petals. Emboss the cup of the flower from the bottom up, towards the petals.

FINISH

Cut out along the outer edge. Place inside the aperture of the paperweight, the painted side facing you. Cut a piece of black card the same size and place it over the parchment paper to cover it. Cover the whole with the sticky-backed felt that comes with the paperweight.

♦ parchment paper, 240 × 170mm, white 150 gsm

Attach the parchment paper to the pattern with the rough side uppermost, using two rolled pieces of low-tack sticky tape.

TRACING

Trace the fold line and the outer edge with a white pencil. With white ink, trace the flower petals, and the rectangular shapes in the corners. Use blue ink for the ribbon, and sepia ink for the rest of the design. Use black ink for the pupils of the eyes, and blue ink for the irises. Trace the rest of the central design with sepia ink.

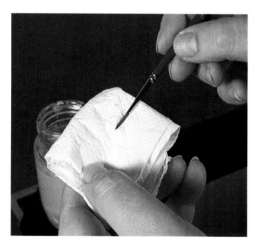

FELT-TIP PEN AND BRUSH – 1

Work on the front of the parchment paper, with the rough side uppermost.

For the hair: draw a stripe of yellow over the upper part of the hair, and a little brown on the fringe. With a damp No.2 brush, using the scrub technique, gently paint the hair; place the tip of the brush

against the line at the top of the hair, and push the rest of the brush flat down, as far as the design allows. Paint from ear to ear, then gently lift the brush off. Turn the paper round and paint the fringe, with the tip of the brush against the fringe.

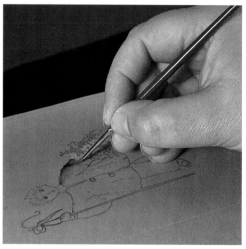

The brown ink should be well mixed in with the yellow.

Use yellow and brown again for the clothes. Starting with the right arm, apply a thin stripe of brown along the

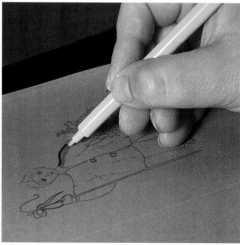

shoulder-line towards the flowers, and then draw a yellow strip just underneath. Using a damp No.2 brush, spread the ink by the scrub technique; using a circular motion, holding the tip of the brush against the outer line, and the rest of the brush as flat as possible, work from the shoulder towards the flowers, then gently lift the brush off. Repeat this for the bottom part of the sleeve.

The brown ink will mix with the yellow ink, and show as a shaded area. Keep this in mind while painting the rest of the clothing, and the leather uppers of the sandals. Paint the buttons on the jacket using brown ink, and then use the remainder left on the brush to do the soles of the sandals.

For the shepherd's stick, apply brown to the upper half, and yellow to the bottom half. With a slightly damp No.0 brush, drag the brown down, and through the yellow. Lift the brush off the paper.

For the ribbon, apply a little blue ink, and use a damp No.0 brush to spread the ink.

Apply brown ink to the flower centres, and to some of the berries. Use red and yellow for the rest of the berries, and, with the tip of a damp No.0 brush, go gently over all the berries, without cleaning the brush between colours. This way, you get a natural-looking blend of colours.

Paint the leaves with a little dark green on the No.0 brush.

For the mouth, take a little red colour from the pen with the brush. Turn the parchment paper over, so that the smooth side is uppermost. With a pen and a little white ink, apply a dot in the corners of the eyes.

FELT-TIP PEN AND BRUSH – 2

Work on the reverse side. Using a skin-colour felt-tip pen and a damp No.2 brush, paint the face, neck, hand and feet. Do this on the smooth side of the paper.

OIL PASTEL

With a rolled paper stump, take a little red from an oil pastel stick. Apply this, very gently, to the cheeks, just below the eyes. Use a clean stump to remove any excess colour.

EMBOSSING – 1

On the reverse side – the smooth side – use the fine stylus to emboss some hairs along the fringe, and a few at the crown. Emboss the outlines of the flowers, the stick, the jacket, the trousers, and the sandal uppers.

PERFORATING – 1

Re-attach the parchment paper to the patterns. Working from the front with the four-needle tool, pre-perforate the border following the grid.

EMBOSSING – 2

From the back, with the picture facing down, use the medium embossing tool to emboss the dots between the perforations, and the rectangle shapes in the corners.

PERFORATING – 2

From the front, perforate the grid again, more deeply than the first time.

CUTTING

Cut the four-hole perforations into crosses, using the fine parchment scissors.

STIPPLING

Place the card, picture facing down, on to the back of the embossing pad, or on a piece of cardboard. With the single-needle tool, prick tiny little holes in the

Exercise 17 – Butterfly Card

For this felt-tip painting and cutting exercise you will need design no. 15.

Attach the parchment paper to the pattern with two rolled-up pieces of low-tack sticky tape, rough side uppermost.

TRACING

Trace the fold line with white pencil. With white ink, trace the scalloped border design. Trace the bull rushes in sepia ink, the leaves in light green ink, and the dots in the border and the butterfly in gold ink.

Detach the parchment paper from the pattern and turn it over.

FELT-TIP PEN AND BRUSH

Working on the back of the parchment paper, apply brown ink to the stems of the bull rushes, and brown and yellow dots to the tops. Gently stipple with a dryish brush to mix the two colours. Draw stripes of light green and dark green ink on the leaves. With a moistened No.2 brush, paint down from the top of the leaves, placing the tip of the brush on the paper first, then applying slight pressure, and gently lifting it off at the bottom.

Dampen a No.2 brush. Apply a stripe of turquoise ink along the top line, and a little at the bottom of the large butterfly wings, then a couple of stripes of fuchsia ink in the centre of the wing.

Using the damp brush, paint the wing with the scrub technique, moving the brush in a circular motion. Starting from the body, paint towards the tip of the wing, with the tip of the brush touching the upper line and the rest of the brush pushed down as far as the design allows, mixing both colours as

centres of the small flowers in the corners. Stipple, free-hand, opposite V-shapes in both corners, trailing from the flowers, and roof-like shapes over all the pointed decorations in the border. Do a little stippling in and around the bouquet of flowers, too.

FINISH

To finish the card, score the fold line, along a ruler, using the medium ball embossing tool. Fold the card. You may wish to use oil pastels for a bit of background colour, or you could use a coloured insert. Trim round edges.

you go. When you come to the tip of the wing, re-adjust the paper and repeat, painting from the tip of the wing back to the body.

For the bottom wings, use fuchsia ink, plus a little turquoise. Paint as above.

Apply brown ink to the body, and the skin colour to the dots in the wings and on the tendrils.

OIL PASTEL

Fold a piece of kitchen paper to a point, and apply a little white spirit. Rub fuchsia oil pastel on to the tip of the folded paper, and transfer the colour to the inner part of the border, and to the corner underneath the butterfly. Apply some of the remaining colour to the centre of the card, just above the water line.

With blue oil pastel, colour the area above and below the purple colour, in the centre of the card.

PERFORATING – 2

Re-attach the parchment paper to the pattern. Using the four-needle tool, and the perforating mat, lightly perforate the four-hole combinations through both layers. The slots are perforated in the same way, but you will achieve a much neater result if you proceed by pricking only one set of two vertical holes at a time.

EMBOSSING

Working on the reverse side of the paper with the medium ball tool, and using the embossing pad, emboss the dots, the top of the bull rushes, and the scalloped decorations in the border.

Using the extra-small ball tool, emboss the bottom half of the dots in the wings and the tendrils.

Working from the front, emboss between the tramlines in the wings.

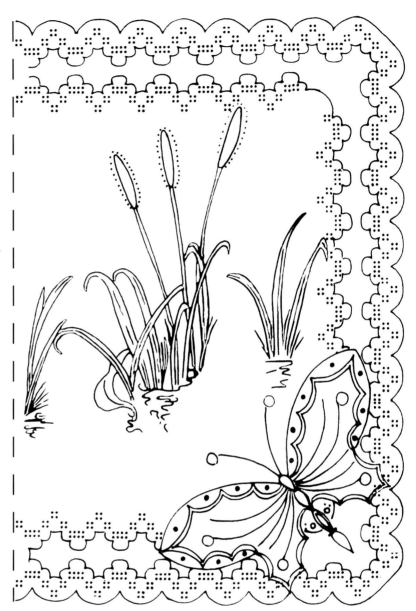

Design no. 15.

PERFORATING – 2

Repeat perforating with the four-needle tool, only this time the needles will travel their full length. This not only stretches the holes to the minimum size required, to pass the points of the scissors through, it will also tidy them up, as, by handling the paper while embossing, the tiny holes may have closed up.

PERFORATING – 3

Open out the card and place it on the perforating mat with the parchment uppermost.

Perforate as indicated, along the upper line of the large wings, using the double-needle tool, pricking through both layers.

Remove the insert, perforate along the bottom line of the large wings, and the bottom line of the small wings. At the bottom of the body, prick three holes between the third and last section.

CUTTING – 1

With the fine parchment scissors, cut the four-hole combinations to crosses and slots (*see* page 40 for the technique).

Score the fold line of the card along a ruler, and the medium ball tool. Fold the card.

Insert a folded piece of blue paper slightly larger than the parchment card, and keep this in place with two pieces of rolled sticky tape.

CUTTING – 2

With the fine parchment scissors, cut the dams between the perforations of the upper line of the large wings of both papers.

Replace the insert snugly inside the card. Hold the card and the insert at the corner, index finger inside holding the insert, thumb on top of butterfly. Gently slip the insert through the slots in the parchment card, so that the blue paper just shows.

PERFORATING – 4

Place the folded card, with the insert inside, on the perforating mat. With the double-needle tool, perforate as indicated, along the outside of the border, through the four layers of paper.

CUTTING – 3

Separate the card and the insert. With the fine parchment scissors, cut the dams between the perforations of both cards. Discard the waste paper.

FINISH

Replace the insert and gently pull the perforated slots through the slots in the parchment card.

Exercise 18 – Christmas: Bells and Baubles

As well as the usual equipment, for this cutting exercise you will need:

◆ design no. 16

◆ parchment paper, 195 × 160mm, white 150 gsm

Attach the parchment paper, rough side uppermost, to the pattern.

TRACING

Trace the fold line and outer border with white pencil. With white ink, trace the

Design no. 16.

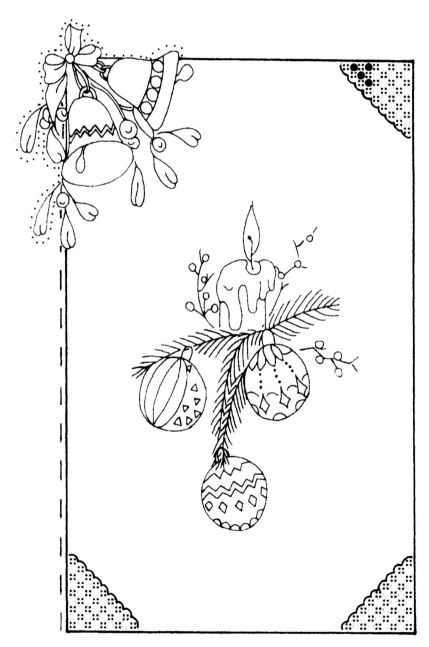

candle, the
flame, and the border
of the card. With white pearlescent ink, trace the small scallops in the corner decorations, and the small rings. Using silver ink, trace the baubles, the berries of the mistletoe, and the clappers of the bells. With sepia ink, trace the ferns' needles and stem, the stems on the berries, the veins in the leaves, and the stems of the mistletoe. With dark green ink, trace next to the sepia lines on the stems of the berries, and between the needles of the ferns. Use light green ink to trace the leaves of the mistletoe, and, for contrast, a few needles of the ferns.

Use black ink for the berries near the candle, and for the wick. With magenta pearlescent ink, trace the ribbon, and the decoration in the bauble.

PAINTING

Paint the flame, using undiluted yellow ink. Apply a mixture of neat red plus a little black ink to the tip of the wick, and to the berries. With light green ink, diluted with water, paint the leaves of the mistletoe.

Using blue pearlescent ink and a pen, fill in the dots in the bell, the large diamond shapes in the baubles, and trace inside the silver lines of the bauble on the left. With magenta pearlescent ink and a pen, fill in the zigzag decorations, the small diamond shapes, and the triangular shapes in the baubles.

OIL PASTEL

On the reverse side of the paper, apply a little orange to the flame. Fold a piece of kitchen paper, add a little white spirit, and spread
the oil pastel in a circular
pattern, fading away from the flame.

Fold a clean piece of kitchen paper, add a drop of white spirit, and apply blue oil pastel to it. Use the paper to spread the oil pastel over the rest of the card. Do not go over the orange colour. With a clean, dry piece of kitchen paper, carefully remove any excess oil pastel, or white spirit, which may spoil the card. Leave until completely dry.

PERFORATING – 1

With the four-needle tool, shallow pre-perforate the four-hole combinations in the corner decorations.

EMBOSSING

Work from the back. Using the fine stylus, emboss the outlines of the baubles, the decorations in the baubles, the candle, the flame, the berries, the scallops,

the rings in the corner decorations, and the outer edge of the card.

With the large ball tool, shade the bells, the dots in the bells, the clappers, the candle, the baubles, the ribbon, the mistletoe berries, and the leaves. Use the medium ball tool to emboss the red berries.

Apply the single-needle tool; gently draw lines in between the ferns' needles, and prick holes in the centre of the rings in the corner decorations.

PERFORATING – 2

With the four-needle tool, re-perforate the corner grids, using the full length of the needles.

Using the double-needle tool, perforate along the bells, the ribbon, and the mistletoe, as indicated.

CUTTING

With the fine parchment scissors, cut the four-hole combinations to crosses alternately, leaving every other four-hole combination uncut. This creates a delicate lace finish.

For the bell decoration in the corner, cut the dams between the perforations. This will partly loosen the back page from the front page. Remove small pieces of excess paper.

FINISH

Score the fold line along a ruler, using the extra-small ball tool. Fold the card. Trim the excess paper.

TIP:

Apply some clear gloss varnish or nail varnish to the berries, and the 'hollow' centre of the bauble on the left. Sprinkle some ultra-fine crystal glitter on the bauble for extra effect; it will stick to the varnish. Any excess glitter may be removed by gently tapping on the edge of the card.

5 Painting with Ink

Using the painting technique first with the felt-tip pens should have given you a good idea of how just a small amount of moisture can spoil parchment paper. You will no doubt have encountered the problem of the paper buckling during your practice with this medium, but this is all part of the learning process. At a much later stage, you will be looking at learning to paint with acrylic paints, but first of all, you need to learn how to paint with inks. This might be frustrating to those who want to learn as quickly as possible but, believe me, it is essential to proceed through the different stages. With this chapter, you should progress to painting with ink, as it explains the techniques in detail.

EQUIPMENT AND MATERIALS

There is a large collection of suitable inks available, under a variety of brand names, all of which can be used, as long as they are water-based. Shop around, and compare prices before deciding which ink to buy. A craft shop specializing in parchment craft will give you all the information you need. For the painting in the following exercises I used non-acrylic graphic inks. I used a No.2 brush for all the general painting, and a No.0 brush for the fine lines – stamens, veins, stems, and highlights.

You will need a small flat palette, or tile, to work from. Do not use a coloured or decorated saucer, as this will divert your attention from the colours you are using for your work.

Exercise 19 – Girl on Seat

For this ink-painting exercise, as well as the usual equipment you will need:

- design no. 17 (page 74)

- parchment paper needed: 220mm × 160mm, white 150 gsm

Attach the parchment paper, with the rough side uppermost, to the pattern, using two rolled pieces of low-tack sticky tape.

TRACING

Trace the fold line with white pencil.
 With white ink, trace the hat and dress. Use blue ink for the flowers, and the irises of the eyes, green ink for the leaves, sepia ink for the face, hair, hands, and the centres of the small flowers, black ink for the shoes and the pupils of the eyes, and gold ink for the rest of the design.

PAINTING

Work on the front of the paper. Dilute a drop of blue ink with 3 to 4 drops of water, using the drag technique, paint

Design no. 17.

tiny spot of undiluted brown ink with the tip of the brush. Dab off (do not wipe) on a piece of kitchen paper. Use the drag technique to paint the hair. The overall colour should be yellow, interlaced with strands of brown.

Add a little brown ink to the centres of the small flowers on the girl's hat.

Paint the shoes black. Turn the paper over to the reverse side, smooth side uppermost, and apply a little white ink to the eyes. Painting the eyes, face and hands on the 'wrong' side will give them a softer colour than painting on the 'right' side will.

FELT-TIP PEN

Apply a line of skin-colour felt-tip pen, of medium thickness, and use a moistened brush No.2, to paint the face, starting below the rim of the hat and brushing in horizontal movements towards the chin line. Do the neck, using the ink that is left on the brush, and then do the hands, using a little colour taken off the felt-tip pen with the brush.

OIL PASTEL

Use green oil pastel to add a little shading at the bottom of the seat. Turn the paper over, so that the rough side is uppermost. Using a rolled paper stump, add a little red to the lips, and to the cheeks, just below the eyes.

EMBOSSING

Use the medium ball tool to emboss a dot in each petal of the small flowers; emboss the socks, the dress and hat, and the scallops inside the gold border lines. With the large ball tool, emboss one side of the leaves, the frills of the large flowers, the pleats in the dress, and the small rim of the left-hand side of the hat. The wrong end of the embossing tool is used

the large blue flowers. Paint the leaves with diluted light green ink. Start at the top of the outline of the leaf, painting in a zigzag fashion, pushing the ink lengthwise with the tip of the brush to the other side of the leaf, ending at the tip of the leaf.

For the hair, use a drop of brown ink and a drop of yellow ink. Dilute the yellow ink with water. Fill the brush with the diluted yellow ink and pick up a

to emboss lightly the tops and cuffs of the sleeves and the bodice of the dress.

With the 'star' tool, emboss, free-hand, some flowers in the collar, and in the upper half of the skirt, or emboss dots with the medium ball tool.

PERFORATING – 1

Perforate a tiny hole in the centre of each star or dot with the single-needle tool.

Score and fold the card. Score and fold a piece of blue paper, slightly larger than the parchment card. Open out both papers, and place the blue paper on top of the parchment paper. Adhere the blue paper to the parchment paper, using small pieces of low-tack sticky tape, just to keep it from moving.

PERFORATING – 2

With the double-needle tool, perforate just below the hat, and along the hem of the dress, as indicated, through both layers.

CUTTING – 1

Cut the dams between the perforations, of both papers separately.

Loosen the cut edges slightly. Re-fold both papers. Insert the blue paper inside the folded card, lining up the hat and dress. From the front, insert one finger under the dress, and, gently pull a fraction of the blue paper down, through the parchment card, resting just over the shoes. At the

same time, guide the blue paper through the rim of the hat, using your other hand.

PERFORATING – 3

Perforate with the double-needle tool through all four layers, round the outer edge of the folded card.

CUTTING – 2

Detach both cards, and cut the dams between the perforations of each card. Discard waste paper.

FINISH

Place the blue paper inside the parchment card, and pull the hat and dress back through both openings
Note: The embossed relief effect of using the star tool – a new instrument – resembles an asterisk.

Exercise 20 – Flower Card

For this ink-painting exercise, as well as the usual equipment you will need:

◆ design no. 18

◆ parchment paper, 200 × 150mm, white 150 gsm

Design no. 18.

Attach the parchment paper to the pattern with two pieces of rolled low-tack sticky tape.

TRACING

Trace the fold line with white pencil. Using silver ink, trace the scalloped and straight border lines.

With yellow ink, trace the daffodils; use purple for the central flowers. The stems and leaves are traced with dark green ink.

PAINTING

It is most important to dilute all the inks that you are using well, even 'light' colours like yellow or green. With diluted yellow ink the colour hardly appears to exist anymore, but it will come back with a vengeance when it is embossed!

Apply one drop of yellow ink to your palette and three or four drops of water. Take a little ink on your brush and mix this with some of the water. Paint the daffodils with the drag technique; the tip of the brush is at the top of the petal, now drag the brush towards the bottom of the petal, applying only a little pressure to the brush. At the bottom of the petal, gently lift the brush off.

Make all the brush strokes close together and slightly overlapping. For

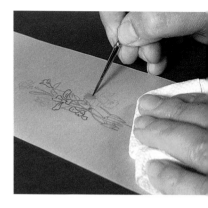

each petal, turn the paper to the right position – the tip of the petal should be at the top in front of you. The same applies to the trumpet of the flower. Turn the paper, so that the opening of the trumpet is positioned at the top.

First paint the upper rim, from the top towards the lower rim, keeping the brush strokes close together. Now paint from the lower rim down, to the bottom of the cup.

Apply the same principle for the smaller purple flowers, remembering to paint from the top of the petal to the base – the centre of the flower – following the direction of the veins.

Mix a little dark green ink with water to paint the leaves and stems as described above.

EMBOSSING

To emboss the flowers, you use the same technique in principle as for the painting. Using the extra-small ball tool, emboss in the direction of the veins – from the tip of the petal, towards its bottom; from the top of the upper rim, towards the lower rim; from the lower rim, towards the centre of the cup. For extra effect, turn the daffodil upside down, and emboss from the bottom of the cup towards the centre.

With the large ball tool, emboss the purple flowers and parts of the leaves. Remember the shading techniques.

The border lines are embossed with the medium ball tool, on the inside of the double scalloped lines. The area between the

straight tramlines is embossed using the large ball tool.

PERFORATING

With the double needle tool, perforate the area as indicated.

CUTTING

Use the parchment scissors to snip the dams between the perforations and discard waste paper.

FINISH

Score the fold line with the fine stylus and ruler. Fold the card, and add a coloured insert if you like. Cut out along outer edge.

TIP:

Prior to cutting, and with the help of a perforating grid, such as a Kombi Grid, you can enhance this card by applying a filled-in, straight border along the outer edge.

Design no. 19.

Exercise 21 – Flower Border

For this exercise, as well as the usual equipment you will need:

◆ design no. 19

◆ parchment paper, 200 × 150mm, white 150 gsm

A border card is a useful one to have pre-made for those occasions when you need a card straight away. This simple design is a good one for people new to the craft; because of all the stippling that surrounds the border design, it looks like a difficult piece of work, but it is in fact an easy card for beginners to tackle.

This card can be used just as it comes, or with a hand-written message, or, in an emergency, a nice text sticker. You could also add a lace decoration or a 3-D ornament.

Attach the parchment paper to the patterns in the usual way, rough side of the paper uppermost.

TRACING

With white ink, trace the words, flower petals and the stems. Use sepia ink for the stamens, and gold ink for the leaves.

Detach the parchment paper from the pattern, and turn it over, so that the smooth side of the parchment paper is uppermost.

FELT-TIP PEN

Apply dark green ink to the leaves. Allow to dry.

OIL PASTEL

Still working on the reverse side of the paper, add some fuchsia oil pastel to a rolled paper stump. Apply this to the petals, spreading the colour slightly outside the boundaries of the flowers.

Use green oil pastel to fill in the area between the flowers, and ochre for the centre of the card.

EMBOSSING

With the medium ball tool, emboss the petals from the outside inwards, starting at one side, gradually moving on to the other side; emboss the words, too.

STIPPLING

Place the parchment paper, picture facing down, on the reverse side of the embossing pad, or on a piece of cardboard.

With the single-needle tool, prick tiny holes, close together, going backwards and forwards in a zigzag manner.

Score the fold line with a white pencil along a ruler, and fold the card.

PERFORATING

Using the double-needle tool, perforate on the outside of the border, as indicated.

CUTTING

With the fine parchment scissors, cut the dams out between the perforations. Discard superfluous paper.

Exercise 22 – Blue Christmas, Round Card

For this ink-painting exercise, as well as the usual equipment you will need:

- design no. 20

- parchment paper, 290 × 150mm, white 150 gsm

Attach the parchment paper to the pattern in the usual way.

Design no. 20.

TRACING

Trace the fold line with white pencil. Using gold ink, trace the large scallops in the border. With white ink, trace the flower petals, and the rest of the border. Use light green ink for the leaves and the fern; sepia ink for the stamens, and the nodules and the needles in the fern; dark green ink for the needles in the fern; black ink for the berries and the stems; and silver ink for the ribbons and the words. Using, consecutively, three different colours on the needles of the fern, gives a more natural look than painting.

PAINTING

For the leaves, add one drop of dark green ink to approximately four drops of water, and blend. Apply a little ink to a No.2 brush and work it into the brush by rolling the brush over the palette; while rolling, gently draw the brush towards you, to 'point' the bristles. Dab the brush on a piece of kitchen paper, to take off excess ink, and paint the leaves in a circular motion. These leaves have sharp points. Start at one end, top or bottom, with the tip of the brush against the outline, and the bottom of the brush as far down as the design allows. Paint towards the next sharp point, remain there for a little while, still moving the brush, then paint on to the next point, and so on.

For the flower centres, use a mapping pen to dot tiny spots of yellow ink on to the stamens; use light green ink for a few small dots closer to the centre, and sepia ink for the centres.

For the berries, apply undiluted red ink; you may wish to use some clear gloss varnish or nail polish to make them shiny.

OIL PASTEL

On the front of the paper, carefully apply light blue oil pastel, using a rolled paper stump and a little white spirit to the ribbons.

EMBOSSING

From the front, use the large ball tool to shade the flower petals, leaving some small gaps for a natural look. Emboss the space between the double lines a little more heavily, to give more depth to the whole flower. Shade the ribbons – use your imagination to show how they flow and curl, and emboss on both the front and the back of the paper to make it look more realistic.

With the single-needle tool held at a slant, draw fine lines in the leaves for the centre vein, and the smaller lateral veins, and add more needles to the ferns by embossing between the inked needles.

Using the extra-small ball tool, or the fine stylus, emboss all of the outlines of the ribbons and accentuate the flower petals in places.

STIPPLING

On the reverse side of the paper, using the single-needle tool, stipple the centres of the flowers, and the areas in the border, as indicated.

PERFORATING

Score and fold the card. Fold a piece of blue insert paper, slightly larger than the parchment card, and slip this inside the parchment card.

With the double-needle tool, perforate round the outer edge of the card, through all four layers.

CUTTING

Separate the card from the insert. Using the fine parchment scissors, cut the dams between the perforations of both cards; discard waste paper.

FINISH

Re-assemble the card and the insert. Use a ribbon or gold thread, and tie the cards together with a knot and bow.

Exercise 23 – Heart-Shaped Basket

For this ink-painting exercise, as well as the usual equipment you will need:

◆ design no. 21

◆ parchment paper, 270 × 180mm, white 150 gsm

Design no. 21.

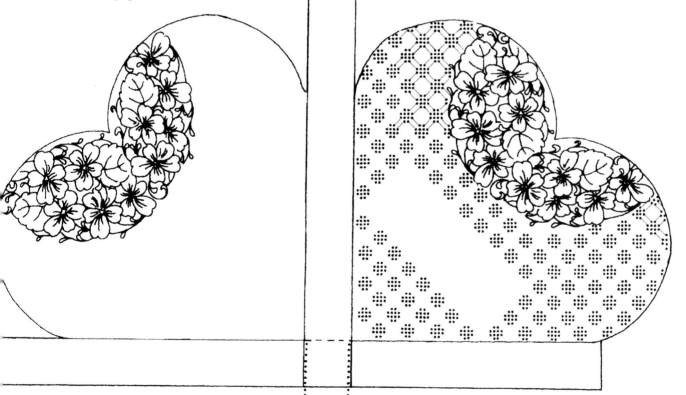

Attach the parchment paper to the pattern in the usual manner, rough side uppermost.

TRACING

Using a white pencil, mark the border, the fold lines, and the scallops in the handle.

With white ink, trace the flower petals. Use sepia ink for the centres, light green ink for the leaves, and gold ink for the words – for example, *Best Wishes, With Love, Just For You*.

PAINTING

Apply one drop of fuchsia ink and three to four drops of water to the palette. To dilute the ink, take some of the water to the ink with a No.2 brush. The ink should appear rather pale; if it does not, apply more water. Now paint some of the flowers, using the 'line-stroke' technique: begin at the upper outline of each petal, tip of the brush against the outline, and draw fine lines, slightly overlapping, down to the centre. Lift the brush off the paper at the bottom of each petal, leaving a tiny drop of ink nearest to the centre. Repeat this with purple and yellow ink, alternating, for the remaining flowers.

Dilute some dark green ink with water, and paint the leaves using the scrub technique. Fill the brush with ink. Dab it off on a piece of kitchen paper. Beginning at the tip of one side of the leaf, keeping the tip of the brush against the outline of the leaf, paint in a circular motion; the bristles should be pressed down as far as the pattern allows, towards the flower, but taking care not to touch it.

FELT-TIP PEN

With brown ink, apply a dot to the centres of the flowers.

OIL PASTEL

Turn the parchment paper over on to its reverse side. Cover an area to be used for your text, name, or a message with a piece of low-tack, sticky tape. Fold a piece of kitchen paper and add a little white spirit to it. Apply yellow oil pastel to the towel and use this to spread the colour over the whole of the design. Remove any excess oil pastel with a clean piece of kitchen paper. Leave to dry completely.

PERFORATING – 1

Re-attach the parchment paper to the pattern.

Working from the front, with the four-needle tool, perforate the grids. To perforate these grids it is best to begin with the top four holes, and come down the grid, 'falling back' to the previous two holes to keep in a straight line. This way you are only moving two holes each time, until the last set of perforations. 'Fall back' to the centre four holes to do the two-hole perforations on the outsides.

EMBOSSING

With the medium ball tool, emboss the petals from the outside towards the base, emboss the centres, and, if you like, some scallops of decoration in the handles. The leaves remain un-embossed, and will therefore appear to be further away.

Using the single-needle tool and a ruler, gently draw short lines between the perforations, as indicated.

PERFORATING – 2

With the four-needle tool, re-perforate only the middle four-hole combinations in the grids.

CUTTING

With ordinary scissors, cut the design out along the outer edge. Make two cuts along the dotted lines, central to the two heart shapes.

Using the fine parchment scissors, cut the re-perforated four-hole combinations to crosses.

FINISH

Score the fold lines along a ruler with the medium ball tool, and fold the basket into shape. Fold the tiny square at the bottom of the vertical handle and tuck it away, inside the basket.

Cut a strip of double-sided tape to the size of the short strip to the right of the basket. Remove the protecting paper on one side of the tape and stick the tape on to the strip of parchment paper. Remove the second strip of protecting paper, and stick the sides of the basket together.

Cut the slits at the top of the handles and join the two ends, so that they are overlapping each other.

TIP:

Use coloured 'Celdes' paper (200 gsm) if a stronger basket is required. For a delicate-looking present, simply emboss the flowers and leaves white, and do the lace work.

6 Bookmarks

Design no. 22.

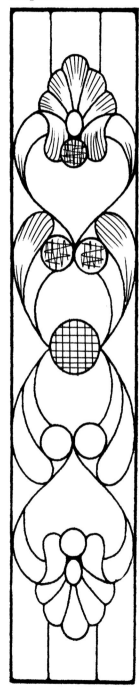

A bookmark always makes a nice present. These unconventional bookmarks can be made with spare pieces of parchment paper, and will not take too long to do. The fun of these particular projects is to use more water than usual, causing some of the colours to bleed into the others.

PROJECTS

Exercise 24 – Bookmark 1

For this felt-tip pen and Kombi Grid exercise, as well as the usual equipment you will need:

◆ design no. 22

◆ parchment paper, 55 × 195mm, white 150 gsm

Attach the parchment paper to the pattern, using two small rolled pieces of low-tack sticky tape.

TRACING

With white pencil, trace the outer line. Use black ink to trace the design. When dry, remove the parchment from the pattern and turn it over.

FELT-TIP PEN

The technique for this exercise is rather unconventional. So far, you have had to be careful not to use a wet brush for painting, to avoid making the paper bubble; this time, you deliberately use a wet brush! However, it is still important not to let the parchment paper buckle, so do not leave the water too long on the paper, and 'siphon' it off by using the rough edge of a piece of torn and rolled kitchen paper.

For this design, the colours yellow, orange, turquoise and purple were used. Apply turquoise to the outer and centre petals of the flowers. With a wet No.2 brush, apply some water to the un-coloured petals; touch the coloured petal with your brush, taking the ink on to the wetted petal. Repeat this with the next coloured petal. The last petal needs just a touch with a wet brush. Soak up any excess water with the kitchen paper.

While this is drying, colour the smaller ball shapes with orange; touch the centres with the tip of a wet brush, leaving a tiny drop of water to blend through. Allow to dry.

Apply purple ink to the centres of the flower; when this is dry, colour the border and the squares solidly, with yellow felt-tip pen ink.

EMBOSSING

Working on the reverse side, use the fine stylus to emboss the single arched lines, free-hand, and the cross-hatched lines, as indicated (*see* page 87).

With the large ball tool, emboss the turn-over leaves and the petals, as indicated.

With the medium ball tool, emboss the round shapes; first emboss in horizontal lines, then the vertical lines, and then go round the circumference. Embossing large circles in this way will prevent the creation of a white 'eye' right in the centre.

PERFORATING

Place the bookmark diagonally on the Kombi Grid, slipping the corners underneath the rim, or using low-tack sticky tape to keep the paper in place.

With the stippling tool, prick tiny holes inside the drop-shapes, using the squares that are showing through the paper from the perforating grid, as indicated on the pattern.

Remove the bookmark from the grid. Place the paper on the reverse side of the grid on the perforating pad, and, with the double-needle tool perforate the corners, the two centre areas, and the heart shapes, as indicated on the pattern.

CUTTING

Using the fine parchment scissors, cut between the dams of the perforations in the corner sections only. Remove waste paper.

FINISH

Cut out along the pencil line. Slip the bookmark into a special 2-in plastic bookmark sleeve for protection.

Exercise 25 – Bookmark 2

For this Kombi Grid exercise, as well as the usual equipment you will need:

- design no. 23

- parchment paper, 58 × 195mm, white 150 gsm

This is another design in the simple but elegant Art Nouveau or Art Deco style. These styles, introduced around the 1880s, and popular into the 1920s, are currently enjoying something of a revival. The styles use only a few colours, sometimes repeated alternately.

TRACING

With a white pencil, trace the outer line. With black ink, trace the rest of the design.

FELT-TIP PEN

The felt-tip pen work is done on the reverse side of the paper. Dark green, light green, yellow and orange were used, but you might choose different colours.

For the lotus flower, use a tip of light green, and a line of orange. Use a No.2 brush to paint the orange towards the green, leaving it rather wet, in order to bleed the colours. Siphon off excess water with the rough edge of a torn piece of kitchen paper.

To paint the buds, first apply light green for the strip across the bud, followed by yellow for the remainder. With a wet brush, apply some water to the green strip in the centre, while the yellow ink is still wet; allow the colours to bleed into each other.

STIPPLING

Working from the back, with the bookmark placed on a piece of board, use the stippling tool to prick, as indicated on the pattern, inside the little circle at the bottom of the lotus flower, and in the yellow areas of the buds.

EMBOSSING

With the fine stylus, emboss the tips of the petals and leaves. With the wrong

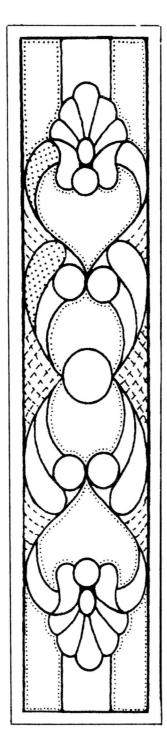

end of the embossing tool, emboss the bottom of the leaves.

PERFORATING WITH THE KOMBI GRID

Place the bookmark diagonally on the perforating grid, lined up with the lines in the wire grid, and slip one corner underneath the plastic rim. Prick holes using the stippling tool, following the grid.

FINISH

Cut the bookmark out along the pencil line, and slip it into a 2-in plastic bookmark sleeve. If you cut the bookmark out along the black ink line, it will fit into a 1½-in plastic bookmark sleeve.

EXERCISE 26 – Cat and Bees

The following design has a border pattern for which we are using the Kombi Grid. The best way to translate the grid for the border is by counting the dots, which I have done for you, so it couldn't be easier! If you do not possess a perforating grid and still wish to use this border design, you can perforate using the single needle tool, perforating through both the parchment paper and the pattern, or,

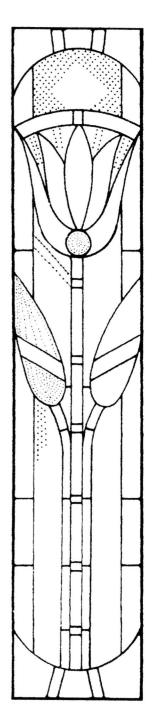

Design no. 23.

Design no. 24.

you may wish to trace the dots with white, gold or pearlescent ink, and then emboss to finish.

◆ design no. 24

◆ parchment paper, 240mm × 190mm, white 150gsm

TRACING

Trace the fold line with white pencil and ruler. With white ink trace the area between the cat's nose and neck, and his front paw. Trace with black ink the fur, the nails, and the bees (but not the wings). Fill in the bees' heads with black ink.

Use fuchsia ink for the tiny petal-formed shapes, underneath the flowers.

FELT-TIP PEN

All painting is done from the front: leave the parchment paper attached to the pattern. Using the felt-tip pens, apply a small dot of turquoise, green and brown ink onto the leaves. Spread this with a damp brush No.1, lengthwise, from one side of the leave to the other side, this way the colours blend, leaving a strikingly soft green, brownish colour, in tune with the rest of the colours that we are using.

For the flowers: try a mixture of fuchsia and purple, spreading the ink from the fuchsia into the purple. The stamens are coloured using a little yellow ink from the pen onto the brush, as we need only a fraction of colour here. Apply a thin line of brown ink over the stem; spread the ink by using the tip of the brush.

With white pencil, draw fine lines into the cat's white fur. Draw a stripe of brown ink on the top of the head. Spread this with brush No.2 towards the white edge. Use the tip of brush No.1 to drag some fine brown lines into the white fur.

Apply stripes of brown ink to the traced lines in the rest of the coat, now with the tip of brush No.2, work at the fur in ultra-fine lines. Add a little brown to the mouth, and light green to the eye, using the tip of a brush.

The bees are coloured by taking orange ink with a damp brush No.2 from a felt-tip pen. Use a little grey oil pastel or pencil for the wings.

KOMBI GRID

Mark the fold line with white pencil. Place the parchment paper on the Kombi Grid, with the fold line square to the lines in the perforating grid.

With the stippling tool (round), or a 'diamond tool' (square) perforate a zigzag line of 10.5 cm. Starting with going five up, and five down, including the one at the top, you should have ten consecutive triangular shapes on your last down-stroke.

To go round the corner; carry on with four more perforations, then come down with five counts and so on, till the next corner.

Fill up the triangles with further perforations, finishing with a straight line.

EMBOSSING

From the reverse side of the parchment paper, using the large ball tool emboss the flowers and the bees. Use the fine stylus for the wings, gently embossing from the body outwards.

Apply the wrong end of the embossing tool for the cat, taking into consideration that a sitting cat has lots of loose skin down his cheeks, shoulders and where gravity strikes!

With the extra-small ball tool, emboss scallops inside the border along the perforations and, with the help of a ruler, emboss a border round the outside of the perforations.

FINISH

Score the fold line using the fine stylus and a ruler, fold the card, and cut out along the outer edge.

Exercise 27 – Art Nouveau Flower in Border

For this exercise, which is a bit of a challenge, as well as the usual equipment you will need:

- design no. 25 (page 90)

- parchment paper, 190 × 145mm, white 150 gsm

The pattern for this design does not exactly match the finished item in the illustration – one has crosses, and one has dots. The point is that you do not always have to copy everything exactly as you see it in the book; you can always change a set pattern. You can mix and match borders and the other features between different designs. You can translate perforating grids into traced dots, and you can also translate dots into perforating grids.

Design no. 25.

TRACING

Attach the parchment paper on to the pattern, with the rough side uppermost. Mark the fold line with white pencil.

Trace with white ink the scalloped zigzag lines inside the border; trace the rest of the design with gold ink. Make sure that the gold ink is dry before taking the parchment paper off the pattern.

FELT-TIP PEN AND BRUSH

On the reverse side of the paper, apply a line of green ink to the leaves, with a damp No.2 brush. Spread the ink in a zigzag fashion from one side to the other, ending at the tip of the leaf.

Apply a line of fuchsia ink to one side of the petals. Paint the petals, with the tip of the brush touching the outer line, and the rest of the brush pushed down as far as the design allows. Move the brush in a circular fashion, from one side of the petal to the other, gently lifting the brush off as you get to the end. If you reach the other side without any paint left, you may wish to apply a little more ink; however, if it is only a tiny area, you might prefer to leave it as it is, as it may look more natural that way.

Use yellow for the trailing tendrils.

Turn the paper over to the front, and apply some fuchsia ink to the centre of the flower.

OIL PASTEL

This work is done on the reverse side. To keep an even line, and to prevent messing up the centre, mask the area that is not going to be coloured, using some strips of low-tack sticky tape. This can be easily removed afterwards and leaves a neat, clean line.

Mask off the area inside the border. With turquoise oil pastel, colour the whole outer border and the places where you are going to emboss later.

Spread the oil pastel to an even colour with a folded piece of kitchen paper and a drop of white spirit.

Remove the masking tape and turn the parchment paper over, so that the front is showing again.

If you want to take up the real challenge of this project, proceed as follows. Replace the parchment paper on to the design. Let the four needles of the tool encompass the dots, making sure that they are absolutely square with the lines in the border.

PERFORATING – 1

From the front, using the four-needle tool, pre-perforate the grid, using only about one-third of the length of the needles. Do not cut these perforations to crosses at this stage. The holes are too tiny and will be stretched by the points of the scissors, leaving the crosses untidy.

EMBOSSING

First, working on the reverse side, use the extra-small ball tool to emboss the white scallops in the border, and the bottom part of the petals.

With the medium ball tool, emboss the outer petals of the lower flower, and also the folded parts of the top flowers. Emboss the flower centres.

Using the large ball tool, gently emboss between the tramlines and the corners, carefully stretching the area all over. Finish with the small ball tool, filling in any gaps.

Use the single-needle tool as a fine instrument to emboss the very fine lines inside the border; going from perforation to perforation, and using a ruler, this can be done free-hand. Use this tool also to stipple the stamens, from the back.

Turn the paper over and, from the front, emboss the remaining flower petals with the fine stylus. Soften from the outside towards the base of the petal with the large ball tool.

PERFORATING – 2

Re-perforate the four-hole grid; this time, go deeper, to at least three-quarters of the length of the needles. The holes will now stretch slightly further, which will make cutting with the fine scissors much easier, and give a neater result.

CUTTING

Cut the four-hole combinations to crosses. Remember, you will save time if you cut all the top two perforations along a row first, then turn the paper by a quarter, cut all the tops again, and so on.

FINISH

Score the fold line, fold the card and cut out along the outer edge.

7 Stocking Fillers

This chapter comprises a few designs that can be used to make brooches. The projects do not take much time, and will make snazzy little gifts. In addition, they use up your spare bits of parchment paper.

Any pieces of waste parchment paper can be turned into many small items, such as brooches, gift tags, or book-marks, and you can also use them to make 3-D decorations for your other work. Simply trace a couple of the same flowers, petals or butterfly wings on to the small pieces, work them in the preferred manner, perforate out, and use a silicon glue to stick the decoration on to your card, or other item.

These brooch designs are not dressed up with 'paper lace'; if you wish to reduce or enlarge any of them, therefore, this should be quite possible, using a photocopier.

TOOLS

- Kombi Grid

- Diamond or stippling tool

- felt-tip pen

- 'Celdes' paper 200 gsm

- black ink for tracing

- design A – small round flower, with embossing

- design B – medium round flower, no embossing

- design C – oval small flower, with embossing

- design D – semi-circle, large oval flower, no embossing

- design E – large round, Art Nouveau face, no embossing

SMALL ROUND FLOWER – A

Trace the pattern on the front of a small piece of blue 'Celdes' paper. On the reverse side, emboss the thin leaves with the small ball tool. Turn the paper over, and shade, from the front, the diamond shapes between the thin leaves. Place

Design A.

the parchment, with the traced side uppermost, diagonal to the design on the perforating grid. Hold in place with low-tack sticky tape. Perforate with the Diamond or stippling tool, as indicated.

MEDIUM ROUND FLOWER – B

Trace the pattern on the front of a small piece of blue 'Celdes' paper. On the reverse side, use brown felt-tip pen for the inner circle, and the diamond shapes. Allow to dry. Place the parchment paper, with the traced side uppermost, diagonal to the design on the perforating grid. Hold in place with low-tack sticky tape. Perforate with the Diamond or stippling tool, as indicated.

OVAL SMALL FLOWER – C

Trace the pattern on the front of a small piece of turquoise 'Celdes' paper. On the reverse side, use yellow felt-tip pen for the centre; purple felt-tip pen for the second row of four petals, and the two outermost petals; blue felt-tip pen for the six large petals between the second row and the outer edge. Emboss the middle four petals with the medium ball tool.

Place the parchment paper, with the traced side uppermost, horizontal to the design on the perforating grid. Hold in place with low-tack sticky tape. Perforate with the Diamond or stippling tool, as indicated.

Design C.

SEMI-CIRCLE, OVAL FLOWER – D

Trace the pattern on the front of a small piece of orange 'Celdes' paper. On the reverse side, use brown felt-tip pen for the second row of petals, and dark green plus light green felt-tip pen alternately for the remaining petals. Stipple the centre of the flower with the single-needle tool. Place the parchment paper, with the traced side uppermost, horizontal to the design on the perforating grid. Hold in place with low-tack sticky tape. Perforate with the Diamond or the stippling tool, as indicated.

Design B.

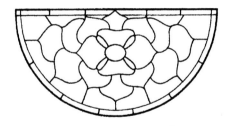

LARGE ROUND, ART NOUVEAU FACE – E

Trace the pattern on the front of a small piece of lilac 'Celdes' paper. On the reverse side, use felt-tip pen, either in the colours of your choice, or as shown in the illustration. Place the parchment paper, with the traced side uppermost, horizontal to the design on the perforating grid. Hold in place with low-tack sticky tape. Perforate with the Diamond or stippling tool, as indicated.

CONCLUSION

I have enjoyed writing this book very much. It has been a really useful exercise for me to think through the basic techniques step by step, and giving instruction also seems to lead to a wealth of new ideas. I hope that you have enjoyed reading it, and that you have gained enough confidence to tackle all the projects; they have all, even the more difficult ones, been very carefully chosen with the beginner in mind.

Following this basic introduction to this wonderful craft, I suggest you experiment as much as you can. With the increasing variety of tools, colouring media and techniques that have recently become available, there is always something new to experience. And do not be discouraged if you make mistakes – simply learn from them, and keep practising.

You might also like to enrol in a course, where you will learn from the experience of a qualified parchment craft tutor. A number of such tutors are currently available, and new tutors are being trained all the time. On a course, you will have help at hand, and this is of invaluable benefit to those students who wish to get really deeply involved in this craft.

For further information, you may wish to contact The Cornwall Academy for Parchment Craft, or *Perga News*, a bi-monthly newsletter of at least 16 pages, with tips, hints, patterns with coloured pictures and techniques, and 'What's On and Where to Go' information. They can be contacted at: Morvoren, Parkenhead Lane, Trevone Bay, Padstow, Cornwall PL28 8QH.

Design D (left).

Design E (left).

Index